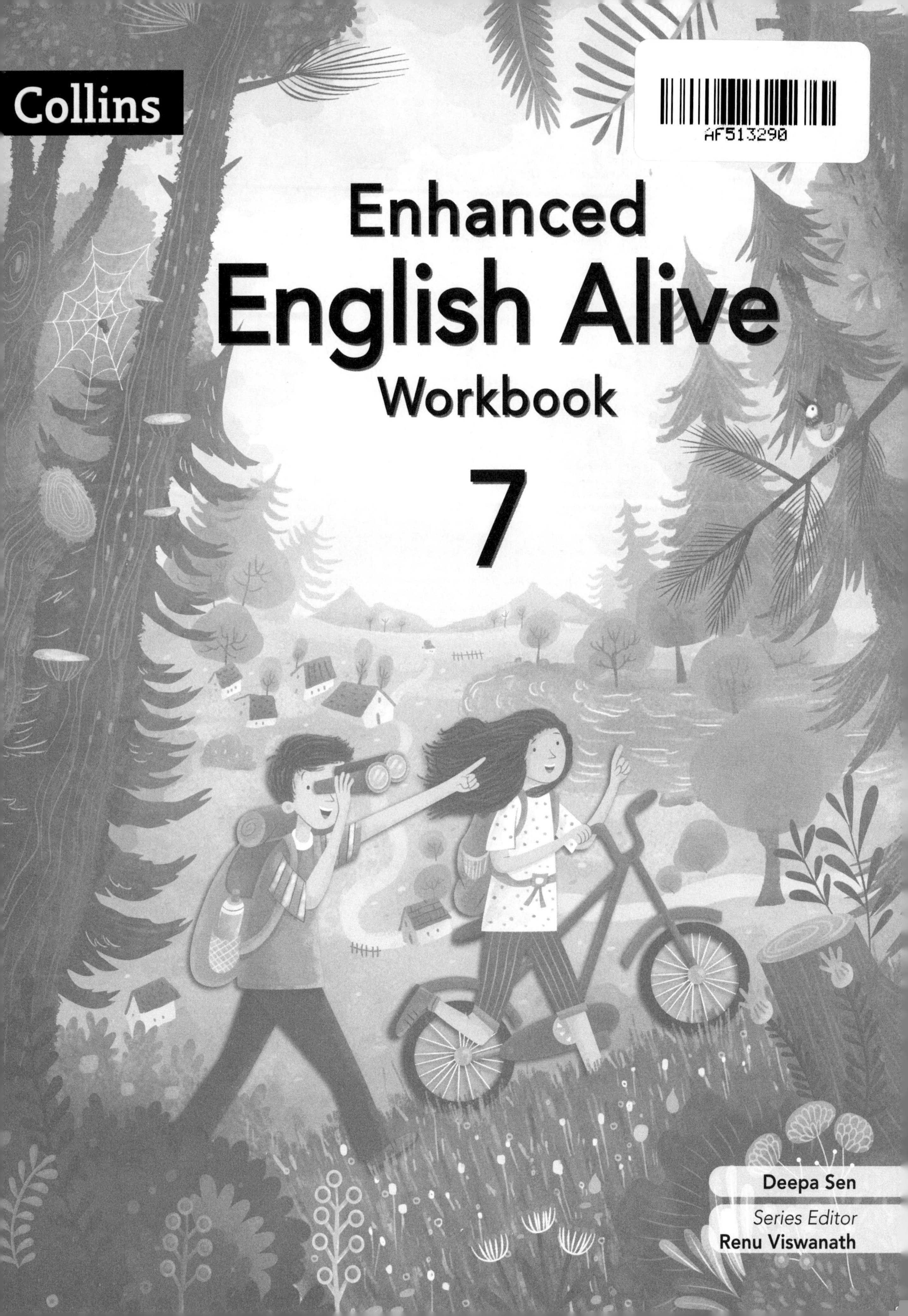

Collins



# Enhanced English Alive Workbook 7

Deepa Sen

*Series Editor*
Renu Viswanath

# Acknowledgements

The publishers have applied for permission for the following:

'The Great Barrier Reef 's Slow Death', published in *https://www.indiatoday.in/education-today/gk-current-affairs/story/great-barrier-reef-larvae-1096762-2017-11-30*, *A Cloud of Trash* by Karanjeet Kaur.
Acknowledgments for the above will be made in the future editions of the book.

Every effort has been made to trace copyright holders and to obtain their permission for the use of copyright material. However, in some instances, we have been unable to trace the owners of the copyright pieces published here. The authors and publishers will gladly receive any information enabling them to rectify any error or omission in subsequent editions.

**Cover and Title Page:** Created by Toonfantasy

**Inside:** Page **15**: VectorMoon/iStockphoto; **17**: Smartboy10, Stevegraham

# Preface

***Enhanced English Alive*** is a multi-skill course in English that adheres to the guidelines laid down by the **National Education Policy, 2020**. This edition retains the original essence of teaching communicative English using a cross-curricular approach and interactive and experiential teaching and learning methods. It offers high-quality English language materials with a coherent structured approach, effective integration of subject knowledge and life skills.

The series comprises Coursebooks and Workbooks for Foundational Stage (Nursery, LKG, UKG, Classes 1 and 2), Preparatory Stage (Classes 3 to 5), and Middle Stage (Classes 6 to 8). Literature Readers are for the Preparatory and Middle Stages (Classes 3 to 8). Each grade package includes a Teacher's Resource Pack and a Collins DigiSuite.

This series integrates the essence of **NIPUN Bharat** guidelines, which extensively deal with foundational literacy and numeracy. Each book aims to motivate learners to read independently, to improve their vocabulary, to develop their critical thinking and creative skills, as well as to enhance their ability to express themselves both verbally and in writing.

This series takes care of the requirements of **Structured Assessments For Analyzing Learning (SAFAL)**. Research-based activities and projects have been used to instill inquiry-based learning, while comprehension passages have been followed by extrapolative and value-based questions that involve analysis-based learning.

## Key features

### Coursebooks

Each Coursebook has a wide variety of texts from various genres carefully selected from both Indian and Western literature. The books aim at cross-curricular teaching, covering topics included in the syllabus of other subjects taught in the respective grades. They also inculcate mindfulness in learners in the Foundational and Preparatory stages (Classes 1 to 5), in addition to language skills. A lot of interesting and engaging activities are used as tools to teach language skills. Additionally, in the Middle Stage (Classes 6 to 8), an end-of-year Assessment Paper has been provided.

### Workbooks

- **Reading:** Each Workbook has 8 to 11 comprehension passages which include prose and poems. Exercises with a variety of questions follow these passages and aim to provide ample practice for the learners.
- **Vocabulary:** A variety of exercises and activities on vocabulary topics mapped with the corresponding Coursebook are given to reinforce the concepts. Exercises on spelling and pronunciation have also been provided to allow a thorough revision of these linguistic rules.
- **Grammar:** Grammar concepts taught in the Coursebooks are reinforced with summarised explanations and graded exercises.
- **Listening and Speaking:** More innovative activities and communicative tasks have been provided to practice and improve the listening and speaking skills of the learners.
- **Writing:** This well-graded section has a variety of creative-writing exercises.

- **Test papers:** Short assessment papers provide a great opportunity to the learners to revise the concepts of vocabulary, grammar, and writing taught in each unit. Each paper evaluates the concepts covered in a group of chapters.

## Literature Readers

The Literature Readers teach critical appreciation of literature through short stories, folktales, fairytales, poems, and extracts from classics from the literature of different ages. The summary of each chapter helps in imbibing the essence of the text. Literary devices are also taught along with a glossary of literary terms.

## Teacher's Resource Pack

The Teacher's Resource Pack contain model lesson plans, additional worksheets, and grammar-based projects covering all the pedagogical aspects included in the Coursebooks, along with listening texts and answer keys to all exercises across Coursebooks, Workbooks, Literature Readers, and additional assessment papers.

# Detailed Contents

| Dictionary Skills | Grammar | Listening | Speaking | Writing |
|---|---|---|---|---|
| • Parts of a word entry | • Adverbs (types)<br>• Words, phrases and clauses | • Listening to a passage and answering questions | | • Formal letter (thanking someone) |
| • Use of *-able* and *-ible* | • Agreement of subject and verb<br>• Use of *for* and *since* | | • Expressing an opinion | • Writing a speech |
| | | | | • Poster making |
| • Abbreviations and acronyms | • Transitive and intransitive verbs<br>• Direct and indirect objects<br>• Types of conjunctions | • Listening and filling in information | | • Writing a descriptive account |
| | • Affirmative and negative sentences<br>• Determiners | | • Making suggestions<br>• *Pronunciation*: words with silent letters | • Writing a newspaper article |
| | | | | • Creative writing: poem |
| • Word origins: foreign and Indian | • Finite and non-finite verbs (infinitives, participles and gerunds) | • Listening and making notes | | • Writing a summary |
| | • Direct and indirect speech<br>• Reporting verbs | | • Persuading someone<br>• *Pronunciation*: syllables<br>• Word stress | • Writing a short story |
| | • Perfect tenses<br>• Prepositions | • Listening and marking true or false | | • Biography |
| | | | • Congratulating someone | • Notice writing |
| • Derivatives | • Simple, complex and compound sentences (transformation of sentences)<br>• *Punctuation*: semicolon and colon | • Listening and completing sentences | • Reader's Theatre<br>• *Pronunciation*: sentence stress | • Making a travel brochure |
| | | | | • Writing tweets |
| | • Main and subordinate clauses<br>• Relative clauses | • Listening and matching causes and effects | | • Report writing |
| • Compound words | • Active and passive voice<br>• *If* conditionals<br>• *If only* and *I wish*<br>• Conditional sentences without *if* | | • Narrating an incident | • Diary entry |
| | | | • Dialogue | |

# Contents

# 1 The Shopping List Mystery

## READING

**Read about how a girl's love of music helps her overcome her shyness.**

### Beth Finds Music

Beth longed for the grand piano, but she could not pluck up the courage to go to Mr Laurence's house. Her sister Meg called it the 'Mansion of Bliss'. She went once with Jo, but the old gentleman stared at her very hard from under his heavy eyebrows, and said, 'Hey!' very loud. He frightened her so much that she told her mother that her 'feet chattered on the floor'. She had declared then that she would never go there any more, not even for the dear piano.

Later when he heard of her weakness, Mr Laurence set about mending matters. During one of his brief house calls, he cleverly led the conversation towards music, talking about great singers whom he had seen, fine organs he had heard, and so on. These stories were so charming that Beth found it impossible to stay in her distant corner, but crept nearer and nearer, fascinated. At the back of his chair she stopped, and stood listening, with her great eyes wide open and her cheeks red with excitement. Taking no notice of her, Mr Laurence talked about his son Laurie's lessons and teachers; and as if the idea had just occurred to him, he said to Mrs March:

'The boy neglects his music now and I'm glad of it, as he was getting too fond of it. But the piano suffers for want of use. Wouldn't some of your girls like to run over, and practise on it now and then, just to keep it in tune?'

Beth took a step forward, and pressed her hands tightly together to keep from clapping them, for this was a temptation; and the thought of practising on that splendid instrument quite took her breath away. Before Mrs March could reply, Mr Laurence went on, 'They need not see or speak to anyone, but run in at any time: for I'm shut in my study at the other end of the house, Laurie is out a great deal and the servants are never near the drawing room after nine o'clock.'

He rose up, as if going, and Beth made up her mind to speak. A little hand slipped into his and Beth looked up at him with a face full of gratitude, yet in her own timid way.

'Are you the musical girl?' he asked as he looked down at her kindly.

'I'm Beth. I love the piano dearly and I'll come if you are sure nobody will hear me, or be disturbed by the sound,' she added, trembling at her own boldness as she spoke.

'Not a soul, my dear. The house is empty half the day. I shall be obliged to you.'

'How kind you are sir!' Beth blushed like a rose. She was not frightened now and gave the big hand a grateful squeeze, for the precious gift he had given her. The old gentleman slowly stroked the hair on her forehead, saying in a tone few had heard,

'I had a little girl once, with eyes like these. God bless you my dear!' and away he went.

Beth was rapturous after that. Next morning, after two or three attempts, she finally went inside Mr Laurence's house.

At last, she touched the great instrument and straightaway forgot her fear, herself and everything else but the unspeakable delight which music gave her, for it was like the voice of a beloved friend.

*(Excerpted from 'Little Women' by Louisa May Alcott)*

## COMPREHENSION

**A. Mark the sentences as true (T) or false (F).**

1. Beth had her own piano. ☐
2. Beth was not a very healthy child. ☐
3. Mr Laurence's visit to Mrs March's house was a casual one. ☐
4. Mr Laurence cleverly tried to attract Beth's attention. ☐
5. Beth wanted to cause disturbance when she played the piano. ☐
6. The only one among the sisters who was very fond of music was Beth. ☐
7. Beth smartly walked into the 'Mansion of Bliss' next morning. ☐

**B. Answer the questions in brief.**

1. Why was Beth frightened?

........................................................................................................................

........................................................................................................................

2. What was Mr Laurence's attitude towards Larry playing the piano?

..............................................................................................................................

..............................................................................................................................

3. What reason did Mr Laurence give for asking one of the girls to play the piano?

..............................................................................................................................

..............................................................................................................................

4. What interested Beth in the conversation between Mr Laurence and her mother?

..............................................................................................................................

..............................................................................................................................

5. Why did Mr Laurence stroke Beth's hair?

..............................................................................................................................

..............................................................................................................................

6. Why did the old gentleman say that the house was empty half the day?

..............................................................................................................................

..............................................................................................................................

7. Find words or phrases in the passage that mean the following:

| | | | |
|---|---|---|---|
| a. courage | .............................. | d. yearning | .............................. |
| b. delightful | .............................. | e. repairing | .............................. |
| c. shy | .............................. | f. disregards | .............................. |

## C. Think and answer the questions.

1. How do you know that Beth felt an irresistible attraction towards the piano?

..............................................................................................................................

..............................................................................................................................

..............................................................................................................................

2. Quote a few expressions to show that Beth was enjoying the conversation.

..............................................................................................................................

..............................................................................................................................

..............................................................................................................................

3. What was the precious gift the old man had given Beth? Why was it precious?

..............................................................................................................................

..............................................................................................................................

..............................................................................................................................

4. Do you think Beth's love for music gained dominance over her nature? Give reasons to support your answer.

..............................................................................................................................

..............................................................................................................................

..............................................................................................................................

5. Do you think the house turns into a 'Mansion of Bliss' for Beth too?

6. Do you think Mr Laurence is as stern as he appears? Give reasons for your answer.

7. The word 'rapturous' means 'expressing extreme pleasure or enthusiasm'. How do you know that Beth was rapturous the next morning too?

## VOCABULARY

### Mystery Words

- In mystery stories, the suspense is often created by using certain words related to the action taking place in the story.
- In fact, authors build up a tense atmosphere by using certain mystery words.

**Match these mystery words with their synonyms.**

| Words | Synonyms |
|---|---|
| 1. mysterious | a. inkling |
| 2. follow | b. sleuth |
| 3. investigate | c. suspect |
| 4. plot | d. pursue |
| 5. detective | e. prey |
| 6. reason | f. motive |
| 7. victim | g. vanish |
| 8. clue | h. baffling |
| 9. foreboding | i. shadow |
| 10. mistrust | j. conspiracy |
| 11. disappear | k. sign |

## DICTIONARY SKILLS

### Parts of a Word Entry

- If we look up the word *giant* in a dictionary, this is the order of information:
  - 'Giant' is the **headword**, i.e. a word that forms a heading in a dictionary, under which its meaning is explained.
  - Then, the **correct spelling** of the word is given.
  - Then the **part of speech** of the word is given, followed by the **definition(s)** or **meaning(s)**.
  - The **background information** of the word, if any, comes next.
  - Sentences are given to show the various **usages** of the word.
  - **Extended words** formed from the headword are given, like *giant killer*, *giant panda*, *giant stride*, and so on.
  - **Derivatives** such as *giganticness*, *gigantism*, *gigantic*, *giant-like* are mentioned.
  - **Examples** of *giant growth* are given.
  - **Origin** of the word is traced from Middle English and other influences. It might be traced from Roman, Latin and Greek roots too.

**Look up the meaning of any three new words you learnt from this passage in a dictionary. Write the entry for each word, mentioning these details:**

| Word | Part of speech | Pronunciation | Example | Origin |
|---|---|---|---|---|
| | | | | |
| | | | | |
| | | | | |

## GRAMMAR

### Adverbs

- An **adverb** is a word that is used to modify or add information to a verb, an adjective or another adverb. Adverbs are of different types.
  - **Adverbs of manner** tell us how the action takes place. For example:

    *She is doing her work carefully.*
    *The athlete ran fast.*

  - **Adverbs of place** tell us where the action takes place. For example:

    *Wait here for a few minutes.*
    *The children are playing outside.*

- **Adverbs of time** tell us when the action takes place. For example:

  *Do your work now.*
  *He will return tomorrow.*

- **Adverbs of frequency** tell us how often the action takes place. For example:

  *We have guests quite often in our house.*
  *I brush my teeth daily.*

- **Adverbs of degree** tell us how intensely the action takes place. For example:

  *He was too lazy to do any work.*
  *He is wealthy enough to afford a car.*

**A. Fill in the blanks with suitable adverbs, according to the given instructions.**

1. We were going .......................................... (*adverb of place*). During the journey, our car broke down .......................................... (*adverb of frequency*).
2. I was .......................................... (*adverb of degree*) happy .......................................... (*adverb of time*) winning the relay race.
3. The baby cried .......................................... (*adverb of manner*) because it was .......................................... (*adverb of degree*) hungry.
4. Come .......................................... (*adverb of place*) .......................................... (*adverb of manner*), don't make too much noise.
5. I had .......................................... (*adverb of degree*) fallen asleep when my dog started barking .......................................... (*adverb of manner*)
6. My sister is lazy; she .......................................... (*adverb of frequency*) does any work. I tried to reason with her .......................................... (*adverb of time*), but she .......................................... (*adverb of frequency*) listened.
7. Shruti dances .......................................... (*adverb of degree*) .......................................... (*adverb of manner*). So, she was requested to perform .......................................... (*adverb of time*) for the Teacher's Day celebrations.

## Words, Phrases and Clauses

- A **phrase** is a group of words which conveys some meaning, but does not make complete sense. A phrase does not have a finite verb or a subject of its own.
- A **clause** is a group of words that contain a subject and a finite verb. A clause can be a part of the sentence or a sentence by itself.
- The table on the next page shows how phrases and clauses can be formed from words.

| Word | Phrase | Clause |
|---|---|---|
| 1. *red* | of red colour | which is red in colour |
| 2. *joyfully* | in a joyful manner | manner which is full of joy |
| 3. *here* | at this place | this is the place |
| 4. *deserted* | with no people present | where people do not live |
| 5. *soon* | at an early date | a date which is quite early |

**B. Underline the phrases and circle the clauses in these sentences.**

1. I do not know how he did it.
2. I was shocked to hear the news.
3. The king sat on a throne of gold.
4. You may sing whatever you like.
5. The girl who had bluc cycs was vcry attractivc.
6. Neil Armstrong was the first man on the moon.
7. Being in great need, he approached me for help.
8. He lived in a house that belonged to his grandmother.

**C. Complete the sentences with suitable phrases or clauses. One has been done for you.**

1. She wore a dress ...made of silk... (*phrase*)
2. Do not return .................................................................. (*clause*)
3. She does her homework ........................................................ (*phrase*)
4. He read a book ................................................................ (*clause*)
5. The house .................................................................. was on fire. (*clause*)
6. She became so nervous ........................................................ (*clause*)
7. The labourer was carrying a load ............................................ (*phrase*)
8. On Sunday, we went ......................................................... (*phrase*) for a picnic.

# LISTENING AND SPEAKING

## Listening

**Listen to the passage carefully and answer the questions.**

1. In which story does Professor Dumbledore make a comment about music?

2. Who is the main character of Charlie Chaplin's silent films?

3. What do you think is meant by a silent film?

4. Who is Maria in the passage?

5. Mention two memorable musical instances from the film *Titanic*.

6. What are some of the instances when music scares us?

# WRITING

## Writing Formal Letters: Thanking Someone

- **Formal letters** are written to any organisation or a person, in an authoritative position, for a specific purpose.
- They are written for favourable consideration of any request by an organisation or a person of authority. These points should be kept in mind while writing such letters.
    - Start with a note of thanks, stating the issue.
    - Write about how it benefitted you.
    - Express gratitude for their efficient/prompt handling of your request.

**Write a formal letter to the manager of the Oriental Bookshop, thanking him for sponsoring the reading session of your school's Book Reading Club.**

(*Your address*)

....................................................

....................................................

....................................................

Date: ..................................

(*Receiver's address*)

....................................................

....................................................

....................................................

Dear ..................................

Subject: ........................................................................................................................

........................................................................................................................

........................................................................................................................

........................................................................................................................

........................................................................................................................

........................................................................................................................

........................................................................................................................

........................................................................................................................

........................................................................................................................

........................................................................................................................

........................................................................................................................

........................................................................................................................

Yours sincerely/Regards,

................................................................ (*your name*)

................................................................ (*your role in the Book Reading Club*)

# 2 Bob Dylan: The Voice of a Generation

## READING

**Read the poem about the linnet, a small brown and grey bird.**

### The Linnet

Have you heard the linnet trilling,
To discover did you try
What is hidden in her carol—
Does she sing or does she cry?

I am singing like the linnet,
When my heart does pine and long;
Love, and pain, and joy, and sorrow,
All are hidden in my song.

*– Philip M. Raskin*

# COMPREHENSION

**A. Read the lines from the poem and answer the questions.**

1. *What is hidden in her carol*
   a. Who does the poet refer to by 'her'?

   ........................................................................................................

   b. What is meant by a carol?

   ........................................................................................................

   c. What is the tone of 'her carol'?

   ........................................................................................................

2. *I am singing...*
   a. Who is referred to as 'I' here?

   ........................................................................................................

   b. What does he compare himself to?

   ........................................................................................................

   c. Which word points out the comparison?

   ........................................................................................................

**B. Answer these questions in brief.**

1. What is a linnet?

   ........................................................................................................
   ........................................................................................................
   ........................................................................................................

2. What does the poet search for in her song?

   ........................................................................................................
   ........................................................................................................
   ........................................................................................................

3. When does the poet sing like the linnet?

   ........................................................................................................
   ........................................................................................................
   ........................................................................................................

4. What is the poet's song about?

   ........................................................................................................
   ........................................................................................................
   ........................................................................................................

**C. Think and answer these questions.**

1. Why do you think the poet wonders whether the linnet sings or cries?

2. What rhyming pattern do you think is being followed in this poem?

3. When do you think a poet writes poems?

4. Are the poet's songs a true reflection of life? Give reasons for your answer.

## VOCABULARY

### Rhyme Scheme

- **Rhyme scheme** refers to the pattern followed by the rhyming words in a poem. It is a common technique that is used in poetry.
- For instance, in the nursery rhyme, *Little Miss Muffet/Sat on a tuffet*, the ending word of the first line is *muffet*, which rhymes with the ending word of the second line, *tuffet*. Since these are the starting lines, this pattern is called ***aa***.
- The next lines of the poem, *Then came a spider/And sat down beside her* also rhyme with each other. However, they do not rhyme with the first two lines, so this pattern is called ***bb***.
- When alternate lines rhyme, the pattern is called ***abab***.
- Look at the rhyme scheme in this limerick by Edward Lear.

*There was an Old Man with a beard,* ***a***
*Who said, 'It is just as I feared!* ***a***
*Two Owls and a Hen,* ***b***
*Four Larks and a Wren,* ***b***
*Have all built their nests in my beard!'* ***a***

**A. Complete these limericks using rhyming words. Then, write the rhyme scheme for each poem.**

1. There was an Old Man of the East,
   Who gave all his children a .............................. (*good food*);
   But they all ate so .............................. (*a term meaning 'more'*)
   And their conduct was such
   That it killed that Old Man of the .............................. (*opposite of 'west'*).
   Rhyme scheme: ..........................................
2. There was an Old Lady whose folly
   Induced her to sit in a ..............................
   (*a thorny plant*);
   Whereupon by a thorn
   Her dress being ..............................
   (*verb form of 'tear'*),
   She quickly became ..............................
   (*synonym of 'sad'*).
   Rhyme scheme: ..........................................

## Musical Words and Phrases

There are many words and phrases based on music or instruments that we use in everyday speech. Some of these are given here.

| Musical words and phrases | Meanings |
|---|---|
| *strike the right note* | to speak or act in a way that has a positive effect on people |
| *blow your own trumpet* | to boast about one's talents, abilities and achievements |
| *fit as a fiddle* | someone who is in perfect health |
| *like a broken record* | going on about the same thing over and over again |
| *music to my ears* | hearing exactly what one wants to hear |
| *face the music* | when someone has to accept the negative consequences of one's actions |

**B. Fill in the blanks with the phrases listed above. Make other necessary changes. One has been done for you.**

1. The factory owner went on and on about the sad condition of the equipment like a broken record.
2. I dreaded going home for the summer vacation to .............................. from my parents, as I had not done well in the exams.

3. When they read out the test results in class, and I heard that I had scored the highest marks, it was ...............................!
4. Our trek leader was a 50-year-old lady; she climbed every rock and hill with agility; she was as ...............................
5. Madhur talks endlessly about his big mansion, his cars, and his fancy gadgets. He constantly ...............................
6. I don't know how he managed to do it, but Mihir just ............................... and the debate ended positively, with our team winning the trophy for the school.

**C. Match the words in Column A with their meanings in Column B. You may use a dictionary.**

| Column A | Column B |
|---|---|
| 1. vocalist | a. synonym for 'song' |
| 2. lyrics | b. a person who plays an instrument |
| 3. track | c. the high sounds in a song |
| 4. tune | d. the low sounds in a song |
| 5. jingle | e. part of the song that is repeated |
| 6. album | f. a person who sings |
| 7. treble | g. one of the songs in an album |
| 8. bass | h. the words of a song |
| 9. chorus | i. a short tune for an advertisement |
| 10. instrumentalist | j. a collection of tracks |

# GRAMMAR

## Agreement of Subject and Verb

- For a sentence to be grammatically correct, the main verb should agree with the subject in person and number.
- When the subject is singular, the verb should be singular. When the subject is plural, the verb is also plural. For example:

  *Rahi likes to play chess.* (singular subject: *Rahi*, singular verb: *likes*)

  *Mira and Meenu are twins.* (plural subject: *Mira and Meenu*, plural verb: *are*)
- The verb also takes different forms depending on whether the noun is in the first, second or third person. For example:

  *I like apples, but Mohan likes oranges better.* (first person: *I*, singular verb: *like*; third person: *Mohan*, plural verb: *likes*)

**A. Fill in the blanks with the correct options. One has been done for you.**

1. Each of his answers ....is.... correct.
2. Where .............................. (*is/are*) my favourite pair of shoes?
3. Aman and his brother .............................. (*has/have*) gone to the fair.
4. A team of engineers .............................. (*is/are*) inspecting the flyover.
5. Most of the birthday cake .............................. (*has/have*) already been eaten.
6. Either Sonal or Raima .............................. (*is/are*) going to be the new Head Girl.
7. None of the dishes we want to order .............................. (*is/are*) available.
8. Neither my sister nor my friends .............................. (*know/knows*) about my secret stash of toys.

## Use of *for* and *since*

- We use *for* to indicate the period of time for which an action continues. For example:

  *The concert continued for five hours.*
  *She has been staying in this locality for six months.*

- We use *since* to indicate the starting time of an action that has continued till the present moment. For example:

  *Football practice has been going on since 9 o'clock in the morning.*
  *The brothers are not talking since their argument last night.*

**B. Fill in the blanks correctly with *for* or *since*. One has been done for you.**

1. This castle has been open to public ....since.... 1980.
2. My mother has been teaching me English .............................. I was a child.
3. I could not talk to him .............................. he left the party suddenly.
4. Our aunt has been living in France .............................. the last ten years.
5. He waited at the station .............................. two hours before leaving for home.
6. The candidate had been campaigning for votes .............................. the last few weeks.
7. We have a dance drama tomorrow, so we have been practising the steps .............................. the last three hours.
8. Emma has been a member of the club .............................. 2006.
9. It has been raining continuously .............................. the last two days.
10. Where were you? We have been waiting for you .............................. 10:00 a.m.

## LISTENING AND SPEAKING

### Speaking

#### Expressing an Opinion

- When we want to voice our opinion about a certain topic, we use some specific expressions to highlight our points. Some of these are:
    - *In my opinion...*
    - *Personally, I feel strongly...*
    - *It is my belief that...*
- If we do not agree with someone's opinion, and want to draw attention to our own views, we use expressions like:
    - *You might be right, but that was not what I was thinking...*
    - *I fail to see your point...*
    - *On the contrary, I think...*

**You like to listen to pop music, whereas your brother is a fan of Indian classical music. Role-play a conversation with your friend or sibling, expressing your opinion on this topic. Use expressive language to support your opinion about pop music, and form suitable responses to your partner's opinion about Indian classical music. Remember to respect your partner's viewpoint, while stating your own opinion clearly.**

## WRITING

#### Writing a Speech

- A **speech** is delivered by a person to rouse awareness or celebrate any occasion. It is generally a formal talk on a subject.
- To prepare a speech, you should note the following points:
    - Choose a topic of your choice and do a thorough research on it.
    - In the introduction, address the audience.
    - Start your speech with an interesting anecdote or fact related to the topic.
    - State your ideas in such a way that makes the audience think deeply about the topic.
    - Add examples and if possible, use humour or wit to hold on to the audience's attention.
    - End with an impressive statement.

**Read this speech by Namrata Arora about the disadvantages of eating fast food.**

Respected Principal, esteemed teachers and beloved fellow students, a very good morning to you. I am Namrata Arora and today I am going to speak on the topic of fast food. I was returning home yesterday, when I ran into an old friend of mine. Both of us were excited to meet after a long time. He insisted that we go to the cafeteria round the corner. We sat at a table and he ordered his favourite pizza. I could now see the reason why he looked heavier than before!

My friends, what have you brought for lunch today? Your favourite noodles, or a burger, or are you going to buy some fries from the canteen? I can feel your mouth water, but unfortunately all the things that might be good to the taste buds may not be good for our health. Firstly, fast food has very little nutritive value and is harmful for the body. Fine flour, white sugar and cheap oil are just some of the things used for making such food. It might lead to stomach pain, fatigue and a host of other serious diseases in the long run. Besides, a continuous intake of fried food will definitely cause obesity.

Your health depends on your eating habits, so you should follow a healthy diet. So, switch to fresh fruits and fibrous green vegetables which are not only nutritious but also easy to digest. Lentils and homemade food keep you fighting fit and do not make a big hole in your pocket. So, before sinking your teeth into the delicious fries, spicy chaat or enjoying creamy, sugary desserts, think twice. It's your health, you make or break it.

**Now, write a short speech on the topic *Should Exams be Abolished?***

..........................................................................................................................

..........................................................................................................................

..........................................................................................................................

..........................................................................................................................

..........................................................................................................................

..........................................................................................................................

..........................................................................................................................

..........................................................................................................................

..........................................................................................................................

..........................................................................................................................

..........................................................................................................................

..........................................................................................................................

..........................................................................................................................

..........................................................................................................................

# 3 The Gift to Sing

## VOCABULARY

### Collective Nouns

**Collective nouns** are those that refer to a group of people or things. For example:

*The swarm of bees surrounded the pot of honey.*

*The audience cheered for the performers loudly.*

*She was carrying a stack of books to return to the library.*

**A. Fill in the blanks with the correct options. One has been done for you.**

| *geese* | *judges* | *poems* | *members* | *flowers* | *directors* | ~~*eggs*~~ | *students* | *ships* | *people* |
|---|---|---|---|---|---|---|---|---|---|

1. She bought a *clutch* of ...eggs... from the market.
2. The *board* of ................................ was having an important meeting.
3. A *gaggle* of ................................ waddled through the meadow.
4. A *crowd* of ................................ gathered at the spot of the accident.
5. A *fleet* of ................................ was leaving from the harbour at dawn.
6. The chief guest was welcomed with a *bouquet* of ................................
7. The *class* of ................................ was full of excitement as they started for the picnic.
8. The *panel* of ................................ selected the best painting from the exhibition.
9. Piyush became famous after the publication of his *anthology* of ................................
10. The ................................ of the *choir* received thunderous applause from the audience.

### Jumbled Words

**Jumbled words** are word puzzles where one rearranges the letters to form proper words. One should look out for these tricks to solve such puzzles easily.

- number of vowels (*a, e, i, o, u*)
- paired letters like *th, ch, gh*
- prefixes and suffixes like *im-, un-, re-, -ly, -ness, -er* and so on. For example:

*palpe: apple* *teulagrh: laughter* *ervir: river*

**B. Solve these jumbled words with the help of the given hints.**

1. zapzi (food) ..............................
2. nabnaa (fruit) ..............................
3. ovjlai (nature of man) ..............................
4. cmapsciu (vegetable) ..............................
5. dglieth (feeling of joy) ..............................
6. oprstnoiepi (part of speech) ..............................
7. paerolnae (means of transport) ..............................
8. dacpbuor (a piece of furniture) ..............................

## WRITING

### Poster Making

- **Posters** are used for announcing an event or for rousing consciousness about social or environmental issues.
- They should:
  - be visually attractive and contain images/artwork.
  - have catchy phrases and slogans.
  - have details of the event/product/message.
  - use different text styles and effects to display the message.
  - have the name and contact number of the issuing authority/address of the venue.

**As Cultural Secretary of your school, design a poster announcing a play to be staged by the school students as part of the Annual Day celebrations. Mention the title of the play and the date, time and venue of the performance. You can also mention the social message or moral lesson contained in the play. Try to make the poster attractive and interesting, so that it catches the attention of students and teachers.**

# TEST 1

(20 marks)

## VOCABULARY ....................(5)

**Rearrange the jumbled words with the help of the hints given in brackets. Then, write them in the blanks provided:**

1. GLEGAG (a collective noun for geese) ....................
2. STHLEU (a synonym for detective) ....................
3. YDMOLE (a word associated with music) ....................
4. TYHRHM (pattern used in poems) ....................
5. SEAR (word associated with a phrase associated with music) ....................

## GRAMMAR ....................(10)

**A. Circle the phrases and underline the clauses used in the sentences below.** **(3)**

1. Snake bite spreads poison in no time.
2. The *Koel* bird is often heard but rarely seen.
3. For centuries, time was measured by the shadow cast on a stick by the sun.

**B. Match the following adverbs with their types:** **(3)**

| | |
|---|---|
| 1. excitedly | a. adverb of frequency |
| 2. never | b. adverb of place |
| 3. there | c. adverb of manner |

**C. Complete the sentences with the correct alternative given below.** **(4)**

1. I have been watching the badminton match .................... (since/for) nine in the morning.
2. Where .................... (is/are) the pair of scissors?
3. The lady has been waiting for her vaccination .................... (for/since) two hours.
4. Each of you .................... (is/are)special in your own way.

## WRITING ....................(5)

**Design a poster that makes the readers aware of the necessary precautionary steps to be taken to prevent Covid-19.**

# 4 Flames in the Forest

## READING

**Read the passage about a tree telling its life-story.**

### Autobiography of a Tree

First let me introduce my mother and father to you. The soil below is also called the earth. And in this soil I was born. When I first opened my eyes and took my first breath, it was the earth that gave me sanctuary. It was in her fertile soil that I was nourished and fed. And just as a mother feeds her infant, I too was nurtured with love in the lap of mother earth.

My father is the sun. With the light and heat generated by him, he has fostered me with strength, so that my trunk can grow and my branches reach upwards towards the sky.

Living close to me were plants with budding flowers. Many colourful and beautiful butterflies attracted by them, would sit on the flowers. Seeing them, I would rustle my branches in an attempt to draw them towards me. But they would ignore me and only fly to the flowers. Once I asked a big tree, 'Why do the butterflies not rest on my branches?'

'O little one, what would they get from your branches and leaves? Where are the flowers on you?'

I looked at myself and observed that there were leaves on my branches indeed, but not a single blossom. Sensing my sadness, the trees counselled me, 'Do not think poorly about yourself. You are now very young and small. As you grow older, your branches will reach high and then many pretty birds will rest on you and sing melodious songs.'

My sadness melted away.

The tree beside me was tall with stout branches. When he spoke to me, he had to bend his head, and when I conversed with him, I had to raise myself and look up. Yet we were friends. He was almost like my big brother. One night when the wind rustled through me, I shivered in fear and looked up to him for support.

You must be thinking that this is only a tree and what do trees have to fear? But, why not? I am a living being and have the same thoughts and emotions as other living creatures. Once a fierce storm frightened me so much that I thought I would die. One by one, the threatening dark clouds covered the sky. Night fell and a strong gale shook the forest. Sudden sharp streaks of lightning lit up the sky like it was on fire. I hid my face in my branches, trembling, and cried out loud, 'What's happening?'

The other trees replied, 'O silly one, this is merely a thunderstorm. It is important for us trees to be able to face such thunderstorms. Just bend your branches in the direction of the wind. Perhaps some weak twigs will break and a few leaves will be shed, but you will soon be straight again.'

Another time, without warning, my leaves started falling and I became anxious, wondering what disease I was suffering from. Even then my brother trees came to my rescue.

'This is the law of nature,' they said, 'You will shed your old leaves and new ones will take their place. Think of it as getting rid of your old clothes and getting a new wardrobe. Our mother earth receives support from these old leaves. They fertilise the soil and build her reserves, and give us and the earth the strength we require.'

True, in a short time, new tender soft leaves covered my branches. This was indeed my new outfit!

– *Saroj Mukherjee*

## COMPREHENSION

**A. Fill in the blanks with the correct options.**

1. The earth gave the tree .................................. (*water/nourishment*).
2. The sun is described as the tree's .................................. (*mother/father*) because the tree grew .................................. (*strong/weak*) with the sun's light and heat.
3. The butterflies visited the plants with .......................................... (*flowers/fruits*).
4. The different trees described in the passage form a .......................................... (*family/school*).
5. A record of one's life and experiences is called an ............................ (*autobiography/biography*).

**B. Answer the questions in brief.**

1. Whom did the tree live with?

   ..........................................................................................................................................

   ..........................................................................................................................................

2. Why was the tree sad? How did the sadness melt away?

....................................................................................................

....................................................................................................

3. 'Yet we were friends.' Why does the narrator use the word 'yet'?

....................................................................................................

....................................................................................................

4. How did the tree feel while facing the thunderstorm?

....................................................................................................

....................................................................................................

5. Why did the tree think it was suffering from a disease?

....................................................................................................

....................................................................................................

6. Write the meanings of these words.

   a. rustle: ....................................................................

   b. nurtured: ..............................................................

## C. Think and answer the questions.

1. Why do you think the earth has been pictured as the mother of the tree?

....................................................................................................

....................................................................................................

....................................................................................................

2. Do you think the narrator is a full-grown tree? Give three instances to support your opinion.

....................................................................................................

....................................................................................................

....................................................................................................

3. What message do you think the tree is trying to convey when it talks about its emotions?

....................................................................................................

....................................................................................................

....................................................................................................

4. How do you think the tree tries to show the seasonal cycle to the reader?

....................................................................................................

....................................................................................................

....................................................................................................

# VOCABULARY

## Words Related to Forests and Conservation

**A. Match the words correctly to their meanings.**

*afforestation deforestation drought earthquake explosion flood tsunami lightning hurricane*

1. A long period of no rain: ..............................
2. Overflowing of water in rivers: ..............................
3. Clearing a wide area of trees: ..............................
4. Strong shaking of the ground: ..............................
5. Planting trees to create a forest: ..............................
6. A storm with very strong winds: ..............................
7. Bursting suddenly with a very loud sound: ..............................
8. Sudden bright light in the sky during storms: ..............................
9. A long high sea wave formed due to an earthquake under the sea: ..............................

## Compound Words

- **Compound words** are formed by combining two or more words.
- They are formed by combining words belonging to different parts of speech. For example:
  - noun + noun (*tooth* + *paste* = *toothpaste*)
  - adjective + noun (*green* + *house* = *greenhouse*)
  - verb + noun (*pick* + *pocket* = *pickpocket*)
  - verb + adverb (*take* + *off* = *take off*)

**B. Join the words in column A with those in column B to form compound words.**

| Column A | Column B | |
|---|---|---|
| 1. bus | a. suit | .............................. |
| 2. washing | b. up | .............................. |
| 3. wrist | c. stop | .............................. |
| 4. bathing | d. machine | .............................. |
| 5. make | e. watch | .............................. |
| 6. on | f. doing | .............................. |
| 7. world | g. in-law | .............................. |
| 8. sister | h. wide | .............................. |
| 9. wrong | i. board | .............................. |

C. **Make compound words with the given words. Then fill in the blanks with the correct options. One has been done for you.**

| *son* | *water* | *board* | *brush* | ~~*book*~~ | *market* | *ball* | *paper* |
|---|---|---|---|---|---|---|---|

1. He reads a lot of books, so he is called a bookworm.
2. The teacher wrote on the .......................................... .
3. The artist was painting with .......................................... .
4. Today's .......................................... has not been delivered yet.
5. The girl used her .......................................... to comb her curls.
6. The girls were playing .......................................... in the playground.
7. The family danced with the .......................................... at the wedding.
8. The lady went to the .......................................... and found all the things she was looking for under one roof.

# DICTIONARY SKILLS

## Abbreviations and Acronyms

- **Abbreviations** are shortened forms of words often used for convenience. For example:

  *tsp.: teaspoon* *tech.: technical* *ave: avenue*

- **Acronyms** are words formed from the first letters of the words that make up the name of something. They are usually pronounced as a word. For example:

  *RADAR: Radio Detection and Ranging*
  *NATO: North Atlantic Treaty Organisation*
  *UNESCO: United Nations Educational, Scientific and Cultural Organisation*

A. **Consult a dictionary and write down the abbreviations for these words.**

| | |
|---|---|
| 1. astronomy: .......................................... | 6. participle: .......................................... |
| 2. born: .......................................... | 7. plural: .......................................... |
| 3. especially: .......................................... | 8. symbol: .......................................... |
| 4. feminine: .......................................... | 9. usually: .......................................... |
| 5. mathematics: .......................................... | 10. verb: .......................................... |

B. **Write the full forms of these abbreviations and acronyms.**

1. a.m.: ..........................................
2. ASAP: ..........................................
3. LASER: ..........................................

4. NASA: ..........................................
5. OBE: ..........................................
6. P.S.: ..........................................
7. FAQ: ..........................................
8. WHO: ..........................................

**C. Write the acronyms or abbreviations of these terms.**

1. Bachelor of Arts: ....................
2. Indian Foreign Service: ....................
3. National Defence Academy: ....................
4. Non-Governmental Organisation: ....................
5. Save Our Souls: ....................
6. Unidentified Flying Object: ....................

# GRAMMAR

## Transitive and Intransitive Verbs

- A **transitive verb** is a verb which needs an object to complete its meaning. For example:

  *Children like toys.* (*toys:* direct object)
  *My father gave me a pen.* (*pen:* direct object, *me:* indirect object)

- An **intransitive verb** makes complete sense by itself. It does not need an object to complete its meaning. For example:

  *The examination started.*
  *I woke up early this morning.*

**A. Underline the transitive verbs and circle the intransitive verbs in the sentences.**

1. The boys seem excited.
2. My pet cat is called Elsie.
3. I feel quite confident now.
4. The child continued crying.
5. We should respect our elders.
6. This film appears to be interesting.
7. Computers are an invaluable invention.
8. The passengers waited patiently at the station.
9. My mother gave me some pocket money.
10. Don't call me by my nickname in front of others.

## Direct and Indirect Objects

- A **direct object** is a noun or a pronoun that receives the action of the verb. It is identified by asking the question *who* or *what* in relation to the verb. For example:

  *Renu ate cornflakes for breakfast. (cornflakes*: direct object*)*

- The **indirect object** is a noun or a pronoun that tells us *to whom* or *for whom* the action of the verb is performed. For example:

  *She showed us all the gifts. (gifts*: direct object, *us*: indirect object*)*

**B. Identify the direct and indirect objects in these sentences.**

1. We painted the house blue.
2. Please lend me your bicycle.
3. I will finish the chores for you.
4. My friend gave me the class notes.
5. The doctor gave the patient medicines.
6. The waiter served the customers their food at the table.

**C. Complete the sentences with suitable direct and indirect objects. Make necessary changes.**

1. He cut the .......................................... with a knife.
2. Mrs Roy teaches .......................................... .......................................... .
3. The bank manager handed .......................................... to .......................................... .
4. I gave my .......................................... a .......................................... on her birthday.
5. The foreigner gave .......................................... some rare .......................................... .
6. The doting grandmother made .......................................... for her .......................................... .

## Types of Conjunctions

- **Conjunctions** are words which join words, phrases or clauses. They are of three types.
- Single-word conjunctions that connect two or more independent clauses or words of equal importance are called **coordinating conjunctions**. Some of the common coordinating conjunctions are *for, and, nor, but, or, yet, still, neither* and *so*. For example:

  *He was innocent and the jury believed him.*
  *The boy was sick yet he went to school.*

- Conjunctions that connect an independent clause with a dependent clause are called **subordinating conjunctions**. Some common subordinating conjunctions are *while, as, because, since, until, although, even though, as soon as* and *so that*. For example:

  *She could not sing as she had a sore throat.*
  *If you study hard, you will do well in the test.*

- **Correlative conjunctions** are paired conjunctions that connect two or more statements or words of equal importance. Some common correlative conjunctions are *neither ... nor, either ... or, not only ... but also, although ... yet, no sooner... than, hardly ... when* and *whether ... or*. For example:

  *Hardly had she finished her homework, when the lights went out.*
  *You can visit the library either today or on Saturday.*

**D. Fill in the blanks with appropriate conjunctions and state their types. One has been done for you.**

1. I went to the book fair ....and.... bought some story books. (and: coordinating)
2. The servant was not only lazy .................................. also dishonest.
3. .................................. she was quite aged, she still participated in the trek.
4. .................................. you come to my house by 4:00 p.m., I will go with you.
5. She had painted well .................................. she won the first prize for it.
6. He played well .................................. he was not chosen for the national team.
7. .................................. he .................................. his brother was invited to the party.
8. The man was .................................. tired .................................. he fell asleep immediately.

**E. Join these pairs of sentences using conjunctions. One has been done for you.**

1. I felt tired after gardening. I took rest.
   I felt tired after gardening so I took rest.
2. Give me some time. I will finish the work.
   ..................................................................................................................
3. You can get the scholarship. You must prepare for it.
   ..................................................................................................................
4. My grandmother is very active. She is seventy years old.
   ..................................................................................................................
5. You should return the book on time. You will be fined by the library.
   ..................................................................................................................
6. She loved to play the piano. She did not play it in front of strangers.
   ..................................................................................................................
7. I will come home. Do not leave before that.
   ..................................................................................................................
8. The rich man is kind. He is also considerate.
   ..................................................................................................................

# LISTENING AND SPEAKING

## Listening

**Listen to the passage carefully. Then fill in the table below with the correct information.**

| Name of the creatures | Size | Weight of organs | Food habits | Social behaviour |
|---|---|---|---|---|
| | | | | |

## Writing a Descriptive Account

- A **descriptive account** is a piece of writing that describes a particular character or event.
- Keep these points in mind while writing such an account.
  - The introduction should be strong and emphatic.
  - The description should be as vivid as possible, involving all your senses and as the situation demands.
  - You should make use of similes for description as well as for expressing your feelings.

**Read this descriptive account carefully.**

**My Grandmother**

My grandmother is seventy years old, but quite sturdy for her age. She is fair, with rosy cheeks, and a shock of snow–white hair, strands of which fall over her face. Wrinkles crisscross her face, and her eyes almost close when she laughs. She is always dressed in pastel-coloured clothes, and her hair is done up in a bun, and she smells of talcum powder. She sings lullabies to my baby sister. She loves to read and recite poems aloud. She always has a story ready for every occasion. I love snuggling against her at night. She loves me and supports me in every way possible.

**Now write a descriptive account about the family member you are closest to. Mention how the person looks, his/her behaviour, any particular habit, what makes them special to you, moments you have spent with them, and so on.**

............................................................................................................................................

............................................................................................................................................

............................................................................................................................................

............................................................................................................................................

............................................................................................................................................

............................................................................................................................................

............................................................................................................................................

............................................................................................................................................

............................................................................................................................................

............................................................................................................................................

............................................................................................................................................

............................................................................................................................................

# 5 Back from the Brink

## READING

**Read a poem about spring.**

**Spring**

Welcome, all hail to thee!
Welcome, young Spring!
Thy sun ray is bright
On the butterfly's wing.
Beauty shines forth
In the blossom-robed trees;
Perfume floats by
On the soft southern breeze.

Music, sweet music,
Sounds over the earth;
One glad choral song
Greets the primrose's birth,
The lark soars above,
With its shrill matin strain;
The shepherd boy tunes
His reed pipes on the plain.

Music, sweet music
Cheers the meadow and lea;-
In the song of the blackbird,
The hum of the bee;
The loud happy laughter
Of children at play
Proclaim how they worship
Spring's beautiful day.

– *Eliza Cook*

## COMPREHENSION

**A. Choose the correct options.**

1. The old English word 'thee' means

   a. *you.* b. *them.* c. *us.*

2. Bright sunrays add beauty to the

   a. meadow. b. butterfly. c. southern breeze.

3. The perfume that is in the air is because of

   a. the sun's rays. b. the butterflies. c. the blossoms.

4. Primrose is a flower. The collective noun for many such flowers would be a

   a. bouquet. b. swarm. c. tuft.

5. The lark sings in the

   a. afternoon. b. evening. c. morning.

6. What shows that the children are happy?

   a. Their wails b. Their laughter c. Their shouts

**B. Answer these questions in brief.**

1. How does nature's beauty shine forth?

   ..........

   ..........

2. What helps the perfume to spread?

   ..........

   ..........

3. What do you think the 'choral song' refers to? What does the song do?

   ..........

   ..........

4. What does the shepherd boy do?

   ..........

   ..........

5. How is the meadow cheered?

   ..........

   ..........

6. How do the children feel when Spring arrives?

7. Give the antonyms of the following words:

   a. float: ..................

   b. cheers: ..................

## C. Think and answer the questions.

1. Why is Spring referred to as 'young'?

2. What do you think is the meaning of the phrase 'blossom-robed trees'?

3. What is the mood of the season Spring? Pick out words that emphasise this.

4. Music in the poem refers to various sounds. What are they?

# VOCABULARY

## Forming Antonyms using Prefixes

- **Antonyms** are words with opposite meanings. Adjectives, nouns and verbs all have antonyms.
- **Prefixes** are letters added before another word to form a new word. We often form antonyms by using prefixes. Some commonly used prefixes are *dis-*, *pre-*, *mis-*, *in-*, *im-*, *ir-*, *il-*, *de-*, *un-*, *in-* and so on. For example:

  *trust: mistrust* *possible: impossible* *regular: irregular*

**A. Form antonyms of these words using suitable prefixes.**

1. appear: ..................................................
2. controlled: ..................................................
3. convenient: ..................................................
4. legal: ..................................................
5. mature: ..................................................
6. necessary: ..................................................
7. polite: ..................................................
8. rational: ..................................................
9. similar: ..................................................
10. throne: ..................................................

**B. Fill in the blanks with antonyms of the given words. Use suitable prefixes. One has been done for you.**

*appeared* *code* *considerate* *fair* *lawful* *reparable* ~~*responsible*~~ *similar*

1. Ravi is an irresponsible boy who never does his work on time.
2. The damage done by the earthquake is .................................................. .
3. Howling eerily, the ghost .................................................. into thin air.
4. The police were able to .................................................. the smuggler's message.
5. Using .................................................. means during examinations is punishable.
6. What Sharad had done was .................................................., and he was jailed for it.
7. The twins might look alike, but their likes are quite .................................................. .
8. It was rather .................................................. of the young man to leave his ailing mother home and go out.

## Idioms

**Idioms** are groups of words which help us convey our ideas and feelings emphatically. Their meanings are often established by usage. For example:

| Idiom | Meaning |
|---|---|
| 1. *at the eleventh hour* | a. at the last moment |
| 2. *with bag and baggage* | b. with all one's belongings |
| 3. *bolt from the blue* | c. unexpected misfortune |
| 4. *born with a silver spoon in one's mouth* | d. born in a rich and comfortable situation |
| 5. *by a hair's breadth* | e. missing or escaping something narrowly |
| 6. *fish out of water* | f. feeling very uncomfortable |
| 7. *gift of the gab* | g. a talent for speaking well |
| 8. *in a fix* | h. in a confusing or troubling situation |
| 9. *maiden speech* | i. first public speech |
| 10. *turn over a new leaf* | j. reform and correct oneself |

**C. Fill in the blanks with the idioms you have just read. You might need to make certain changes to them.**

1. Richie Rich, the comic character, was .............................................. .
2. Everyone was impressed by the young leader's .............................................. .
3. Lost in the forest, without food and water, Rick was .............................................. .
4. A politician should have the .............................................. to hold people's attention.
5. The criminal promised to .............................................. when he was released finally.
6. Mr Mehta was transferred, so the family left the town .............................................. .
7. At the new school, the child felt like a .............................................. for the first few days.
8. The news of the earthquake hitting the tropical island was a .............................................. .
9. They got the ticket .............................................. and could watch the match live at the stadium.
10. The fireman had escaped .............................................. while he was rescuing a woman trapped in the burning building.

## Spelling

### Use of *long a* and *long e*

- The *long a* sound is used in words with
  - long *a* as in *able, agent, aim*
  - *a-e* as in *bake, grate, imitate*
  - *ai* as in *grain, maid, paid*
  - *ay* as in *may, lay, essay*
  - *ei* as in *weigh, vein, reign*
- The *long e* sound is used in words with
  - *ee* as in *feel, deep, three*
  - *ea* as in *cream, reason, feast*
  - *e* as in *here, these, delete*
  - *ie* as in *sieve, shield, achieve*
  - *ei* as in *deceive, ceiling, receipt*
  - *y* as in *happy, glory, cherry*

**D. Identify the *long a* and *long e* sounds in these words.**

| | | | |
|---|---|---|---|
| 1. feet | 5. me | 9. lead | 13. meat |
| 2. lane | 6. eight | 10. whale | 14. receive |
| 3. eagle | 7. pay | 11. baseball | 15. rain |
| 4. raise | 8. cry | 12. nail | 16. mail |

**E. Make a list of five words each for the *long a* and *long e* sounds.**

| *long a* | *long e* |
|---|---|
| 1. ........................................ | 1. ........................................ |
| 2. ........................................ | 2. ........................................ |
| 3. ........................................ | 3. ........................................ |
| 4. ........................................ | 4. ........................................ |
| 5. ........................................ | 5. ........................................ |

### Use of *short a*

- When we use the *short a* sound, the pronunciation of *a* varies from that of the *long a* sound. For instance, the word *main* has a *long a* sound because we pronounce the *a* as *ay*, whereas the word *man* has a short vowel sound.
- Three-letter words like *act, cat, gap, had, nap, sad, tap, van* have the *short a* sound.

**F. Underline the words with the *short a* sound in these sentences, and read them aloud.**

1. The fat cat is running after the tiny rat.
2. I am glad to write the last exam today.
3. The Andrews have ten farm animals.
4. The last clean hat I have is black in colour.
5. The cats are playing on the mat near my bag.
6. Their bathroom has a leaky tap.

## GRAMMAR

### Affirmative and Negative Sentences

- An **affirmative sentence** makes a positive statement; a **negative sentence** makes a negative statement.
- We can change an affirmative sentence to a negative sentence by using an antonym for the adjective, adverb or verb and by adding a negative word such as *no, not, never*. For example:

  *She always completes her work on time.* (affirmative)
  *She never leaves her work incomplete.* (negative)

  *It is not easy to speak the truth in every situation.* (negative)
  *It is difficult to speak the truth in every situation.* (affirmative)

**A. Change the negative sentences into affirmative sentences. Make sure that the meaning remains the same.**

1. He is never on time for class.
2. I am not as quarrelsome as you.
3. No other player is as good as Piu.
4. No one draws as well as this small boy in the locality.
5. You cannot deny that he played the piano very well.
6. No sooner did the dog enter the room, than the cat ran away.
7. There was nobody present in the stadium who did not clap when India won the match.

**B. Change the affirmative sentences into negative sentences. Make sure that the meaning remains the same.**

1. The film is boring.
2. We should respect our elders.
3. Everyone praised his painting.
4. She is the tallest girl in the class.
5. As soon as the bell rang, all the children rushed out.
6. The naughty boy admitted that he had broken the vase.
7. Only students of class seven can participate in the competition.

## Determiners

- **Determiners** are words used before nouns to indicate which nouns are being referred to. They are either specific or general in meaning. For example:

  *The princess had long black hair.*
  *This letter arrived today.*
  *It is his pencil box.*
  *Each box contains a set of watercolours.*

- These are the most common types of determiners.

| Types | Determiners |
|---|---|
| Articles | *a, an, the* |
| Demonstratives | *this, these, that, those* |
| Possessives | *my, our, your, his, her, its, their* |
| Cardinal and ordinal numbers | *one, two, ten, first, second, tenth*, etc. |
| Quantifiers | *many, few, several, all, some, more, most, none* |
| Distributives | *each, every, neither, either* |
| Interrogatives | *which, whose, what* |

**C. Fill in the blanks correctly with determiners.**

| *a* | *many* | *an* | *the* | *his* | *two* | *our* | *my* | *third* | *that* |
|---|---|---|---|---|---|---|---|---|---|

1. .................................. juicy mangoes hung from the trees.
2. She wants to buy .................................. doll displayed in the corner of the toy section.
3. He invited .................................. friends to the party.
4. This is the .................................. time India has won the Champion's Trophy.
5. .................................. apple a day keeps .................................. doctor away.
6. The school is like .................................. second home.
7. Please give me .................................. piece of cake.
8. .................................. uncle has .................................. houses in Delhi.

# LISTENING AND SPEAKING

## Speaking

### Making Suggestions

Before taking up a work or starting something, you will often find others offering suggestions to you on how to proceed. These are some expressions generally used to make suggestions:

- *Why don't we...*
- *Would you prefer...*
- *What/How about doing...*
- *Let's...*
- *That's a great idea...*

**A. Suggest your friend about what to do after your exams get over and the summer holidays begin. He/She has been thinking about going on a trip somewhere, so make suggestions regarding those plans as well.**

## Pronunciation

### Words with Silent Letters

- There are certain words in the English language in which some letters, though used, are not pronounced. These letters stay silent when the word is pronounced.
- Some rules that silent letters follow are:
  - *b* remains silent after 'm', as in *dumb, numb*
  - *g* remains silent before 'n', as in *foreign, reign*

- *h* remains silent when used after 'g' with a vowel before it, as in *night, fight*
- *k* remains silent when used before 'n', as in *knight, know*
- *l* remains silent when used before 'm', as in *calm, balm*
- *s* remains silent when used after 'i', as in *island, isle*
- *t* remains silent when used after 's', as in *castle, listen*
- *w* remains silent in words like *write, who*

**B. Write two words each with the eight silent letters you have just learnt.**

| Silent Letter | Words |
|---|---|
| *b* | ........................................ |
| *g* | ........................................ |
| *h* | ........................................ |
| *k* | ........................................ |
| *l* | ........................................ |
| *s* | ........................................ |
| *t* | ........................................ |
| *w* | ........................................ |

## WRITING

### Newspaper Article

- A **newspaper article** or report may cover matters or incidents which affect the larger public. It may be a short account about a notable incident, or a longer essay-like piece discussing an issue in detail.
- While writing a newspaper article, one should keep these points in mind.
  - The 5 'W's: what happened, where it happened, when it happened, why it happened, who did it happen to
  - The headline should immediately attract attention.
  - Mention the issue, discussing its magnitude and those affected, with valid examples.
  - Probable causes behind the issue
  - Possible solutions and measures taken
  - Concluding statement

**Write a newspaper article about a performance put up by a troupe of blind dancers. Mention the time and venue of the performance, how the various dancers overcame their disability to deliver a stunning act. Write about the finer points of the performance, the dancers' coordination and expressions, and how they touched you with their spectacular moves. You can also write about what some of the dancers and the audience members said after the performance was over.**

# 6 Birds of a Feather

## VOCABULARY

### Similes

**Similes** are words or phrases that compare something to something else, using the words *like* or *as*. For example:

*Ravi's face was like a mask, not betraying any emotion.*
*She was wearing a dress that was as white as snow.*

**A. Complete the sentences with the correct similes.**

*as thick as thieves*    *as wise as an owl*    *as hungry as a horse*    *as happy as a lark*    *as noisy as bedlam*    *as blind as a bat*

1. Getting the new toy car that he had longed for, the child was .................................................. .
2. Swami and Rajam were .................................................., right from childhood.
3. The class was .................................................. in the teacher's absence.
4. On entering the empty, dark house at night, he felt .................................................. .
5. After hiking the whole day, the man was .................................................. when he reached the inn.
6. Professor Dumbledore from the *Harry Potter* series is .................................................. .

**B. Write four sentences describing the following, using different similes.**

1. your father (*appearance, complexion, nature*)

..................................................................................................................

..................................................................................................................

..................................................................................................................

..................................................................................................................

2. your pet (*colour, size, nature*)

## WRITING

### Creative Writing: Poem

**Imagine a situation that led you to think 'It was a fortunate mistake indeed!' Now write a short poem on this topic, describing how the mistake happened, your role in it and why it turned out to be fortunate after all.**

# TEST 2

(20 marks)

## VOCABULARY ................................................................................................(5)

**Fill in the table below with your answer:**

| | WORD/PHRASE | WHAT TO DO | ANSWER |
|---|---|---|---|
| 1. | Considerate | use prefix and write opposite | .................................. |
| 2. | Fire | make a compound word with it | .................................. |
| 3. | Clear | make a simile with it | .................................. |
| 4. | Hit the nail on the head | write meaning of it | .................................. |
| 5. | seal, gale | identify word with long 'e' and long 'a' sound | .................................. |

## GRAMMAR ................................................................................................(10)

**A. From the sentences given below identify the verbs, state which kind the verb is and write it in the blanks given.** **(3)**

| | Verb | Type |
|---|---|---|
| 1. In early days news travelled on horseback, by sea or through carrier pigeons. | .............................. | .............................. |
| 2. The people use ballots to choose their leader. | .............................. | .............................. |
| 3. The teachers sent the question papers. | .............................. | .............................. |

**B. Fill in the blanks with the correct conjunctions.** **(3)**

1. ..................... had I finished the exam ..................... the bell rung.
2. The mountaineers had climbed the steep slope ..................... were tired.
3. .....................we approach our friends in time if distress, they will surely help us.

**C. Complete the conversation using determiners where necessary.** **(2)**

Shefali: Are ..................... books on the shelf by Enid Blyton?

Shopkeeper: Yes. They are adventure stories of the Famous Five which ..................... children love.

**D. Change the Negative sentence into Affirmative and the Affirmative sentence into a Negative** **(2)**

1. As soon as the leopard saw its prey, it rushed towards it.

 ..........................................................................................................

2. I do not love any comics as much as I love Tintin comics.

 ..........................................................................................................

## WRITING ..........(5)

**Write a short description of your pet. You may write about its appearance, behaviour, habits and what makes it so endearing to you.**

..........................................................................................................

..........................................................................................................

..........................................................................................................

..........................................................................................................

..........................................................................................................

..........................................................................................................

..........................................................................................................

..........................................................................................................

..........................................................................................................

..........................................................................................................

..........................................................................................................

..........................................................................................................

..........................................................................................................

..........................................................................................................

..........................................................................................................

..........................................................................................................

..........................................................................................................

..........................................................................................................

..........................................................................................................

..........................................................................................................

..........................................................................................................

..........................................................................................................

..........................................................................................................

# 7 Fourteen - I

## READING

**Read this story about the adventures of a mischievous crow.**

### A Crow in the House

The young crow had fallen from its nest and was fluttering about on the road, in danger of being crushed by a cart or seized by a cat, when I picked it up and brought it home. It was in a sorry state, beak gaping and head dropping, and we did not expect it to live. But Grandfather and I did our best to bring it round. We fed it by prising its beak gently open with a pencil, pushing in a little milk and bread, and then removing the pencil to allow it to swallow. We varied this diet with occasional doses of Grandmother's home-made plum wine, and as a result, the young crow was soon on the road to recovery.

He was offered freedom but he did not take it. Instead he made himself at home. He took over the administration of the house. We called him Caesar.

He danced about on the dining table and gave us no peace until he had been given his small bowl of meal consisting of soup and vegetables. He was always restless, fidgeting about, investigating things. He would hop across a table to empty a matchbox of its contents or rip the daily paper to shreds, or overturn a vase of flowers, or tug at the tail of one of the dogs.

'That crow will be the ruin of us!' grumbled Grandmother, 'Can't you keep him in a cage?'

We did try keeping Caesar in a cage, but he was so angry, and objected with such fierce cawing and flapping that we thought that it was better for our nerves and peace of mind to give him the run of the house. He did not show any inclination to join the other crows in the banyan tree. Grandfather said that this was because he was a jungle crow and probably felt contemptuous of the very ordinary carrion crows. But it seemed to me that Caesar, having grown used to living with humans on equal terms, had become snobbish and did not wish to mix with his own kind.

In time, Caesar learnt to talk a little, in a cracked throaty voice. He seemed to recognize the click of the gate when I came home from school and would come to the door with a hop, skip and a jump, saying 'Hello, hello!' I had also taught him to sit on my arm and say 'Kiss, kiss.'

On one of Aunt Mabel's visits, Caesar landed on her arm and cackled, 'Kiss, kiss'. Aunt Mabel was delighted and leant forward for a kiss. But Caesar's attention shifted to my aunt's gleaming spectacles, and thrusting at them with his beak, he knocked them off.

Grandmother insisted that Caesar was a pest, in spite of his engaging habits. If he had restricted his activities to our house, it would not have been so bad: but he took to visiting our neighbouring houses and stealing pens and pencils, hair ribbons, combs, keys, shuttlecocks, toothbrushes and false teeth. He was especially fond of toothbrushes, and made a collection of them on top of the cupboard in my room. Toothbrush sales went up that year and so did Grandmother's blood pressure.

Caesar spied on children buying sweets and often managed to snatch them as they came out. Clothes pegs fascinated him. Neighbours would return from the bazaar to find their washing lying in the mud, and no sign of the pegs. These too found their way to the top of my cupboard!

[Excerpted from the story 'A Crow in the House' from *Grandfather's Private Zoo* by Ruskin Bond]

## COMPREHENSION

**A. Mark the sentences as true (T) or false (F).**

1. Having fallen from a tree, the crow was in danger of being crushed by a cart. ☐
2. To help the crow recover, the narrator and his grandfather fed him only bread. ☐
3. When offered freedom, Caesar declined it as he was comfortable staying home. ☐
4. The crow's voice was melodious. ☐
5. The crow swooped on the sweets and snatched it from the children when they were in school. ☐

**B. Read the lines from the passage and answer the questions.**

1. *It was in a sorry state...*

   a. What was the state of the crow?

   ..........................................................................................

   b. What was done to make it overcome its sorry state?

   ..........................................................................................

   c. How do you know the crow became attached to the family after it was treated?

   ..........................................................................................

2. *'That crow will be the ruin of us!'*

   a. Who said this?

   ..........................................................................................

   b. Why did the person say so about the crow?

   ..........................................................................................

   c. What did the person suggest as a solution?

   ..........................................................................................

3. *Aunt Mabel was delighted...*

   a. What delighted Aunt Mabel?

   ..........................................................................................

   b. Did Caesar behave as she expected?

   ..........................................................................................

   c. What do you think was Aunt Mabel's reaction to Caesar's behaviour?

   ..........................................................................................

**C. Think and answer the questions.**

1. Why was Caesar not kept in a cage?

   ..........................................................................................

   ..........................................................................................

   ..........................................................................................

2. Do you consider Caesar to be a pet or a pest? Give reasons for your answer.

   ..........................................................................................

   ..........................................................................................

   ..........................................................................................

3. What image do you draw of Caesar from the text?

..........................................................................................

..........................................................................................

..........................................................................................

4. Suppose your friends have come to your house and see their toothbrushes, pens, pencils, or shuttlecocks there. What would be their reaction and how would you explain?

..........................................................................................

..........................................................................................

..........................................................................................

# VOCABULARY

## Exaggeration for Dramatic Effect

- Certain expressions are used to add dramatic effect to an otherwise ordinary description of an event or a character.
- This is done to make the description more emphatic, lively or comical. For example:

  The expressions *he gave us no peace* and *he will be the ruin of us* are used to describe the crow's nuisance in an exaggerated way.

**A. Underline the dramatic expressions used in these sentences. The first one has been done for you.**

1. Please buy me a pair of new shoes. The pair I'm wearing is a thousand years old.
2. I've told you a hundred times not to forget the keys to the house!
3. She was crying so badly, as if drowning in her own tears.
4. He was very tired after the hectic day. He could sleep for years.
5. I have not eaten anything since breakfast. I am so hungry that I can even eat a horse.
6. This is my favourite programme. I could go on watching it forever.
7. I could not understand the foreign script and the letters danced in front of my eyes.
8. I am meeting my best friend after ages today.

**B. Fill in the blanks with the correct options.**

| *piles* | *ton* | *lake* | *killing* | *stealthy* | *twenty-feet* | *toothpick* | *jet* |
|---|---|---|---|---|---|---|---|

1. She cried so much that her tears formed a ..........................................
2. The beggar is as thin as a ..........................................
3. The dictionary I brought from the library weighs a ..........................................
4. He seems to be almost .......................................... tall.

5. The athlete ran past his opponent like a ..........................................

6. The shoe bite from the new shoes is .......................................... me.

7. The student grumbled saying that he had .......................................... of homework to do.

8. The detective had to be as .......................................... as a cat while following the suspect.

## Homonyms

**Homonyms** are two or more words having the same spelling or pronunciation but with different meanings. For example:

| | | |
|---|---|---|
| *bear: to tolerate* | *fair: carnival* | *current: latest* |
| *bear: an animal* | *fair: just* | *current: flow of electricity through a wire* |

**C. Write the homonyms which fit each pair of meanings. One has been done for you.**

1. to check how many/to rely on: count
2. something to read/to reserve something: ..........................................
3. sound a dog makes/trunk of a tree: ..........................................
4. something to write with/place for keeping animals: ..........................................
5. to speak to someone/exact location: ..........................................
6. a season/to jump suddenly: ..........................................
7. a penalty to pay/good quality: ..........................................
8. type of something/the quality of being caring: ..........................................

**D. Find out the two different meanings for each of these homonyms. Then write two sentences for each word showing the difference in meaning.**

1. well: ..........................................
   well: ..........................................
2. stretch: ..........................................
   stretch: ..........................................
3. right: ..........................................
   right: ..........................................
4. draw: ..........................................
   draw: ..........................................
5. pride: ..........................................
   pride: ..........................................
6. might: ..........................................
   might: ..........................................

## Homophones

**Homophones** are words that have the same pronunciation but differ in spelling and meaning. For example:

*Look to your right before crossing the road. (direction)*
*Write down the names of all the planets in the solar system. (the act of noting down something)*

**E. Fill in the blanks with the correct words.**

1. I would like some .................................... (*plane/plain*) water.
2. .................................... (*Peace/Piece*) of mind is very important for maintaining good health.
3. The contestants should come .................................... (*forth/fourth*) and take their seats.
4. I hope I don't .................................... (*bore/boar*) you with my travel stories.
5. The agency has booked a special .................................... (*sweet/suite*) for our stay in Jaipur.
6. Mr Sen's garden is full of such exotic .................................... (*flours/flowers*).
7. The .................................... (*soul/sole*) of one of his running shoes has come off.

# DICTIONARY SKILLS

## Word Origins

- Many words in the English language are derived from other foreign languages, including Indian. For instance, *verandah* is a word of Indian origin as it did not exist in the English terminology, or *bangles*, which is typically associated with Indian women's ornaments.
- The word *cookie* is of Dutch origin. It refers to a sweet snack made of rolled and baked sweet dough. The word is derived from the Dutch term *koekie* which is defined as something like a cake.
- Again, the word *cartoon* is of Italian origin. It refers to a sketch or a drawing showing humorous situations. It is derived from the Italian word *carton* which initially meant a drawing on hard paper, and the meaning later changed to a comical presentation.

**Some words of foreign and Indian origin in English are listed below. Look up the dictionary and trace their origins.**

1. ballet: ....................................
2. bungalow: ....................................
3. café: ....................................
4. cigar: ....................................
5. entrepreneur: ....................................
6. jungle: ....................................
7. loot: ....................................

8. metropolis: ..........................................................................................

9. origami: ..........................................................................................

10. rucksack: ..........................................................................................

11. shampoo: ..........................................................................................

12. typhoon: ..........................................................................................

# GRAMMAR

## Finite and Non-Finite Verbs

- **Finite verbs** are those that change their form according to the number and person of the subject of the sentence. They have present, past and future forms. For example:

  *I am going to my cousin's house in the evening.*
  *Vinod and Saurav play football in the weekends.*

- Finite verbs indicate the tense of the verb and the person and number of the subject. They must agree with the subject and can be in the active or passive voice.
- **Non-Finite verbs** are those that do not change their form according to the number and person of the subject of the sentence. They do not indicate tense and function as nouns and adjectives. For example:

  *The burglar tried to open the safe.*
  *Painting landscapes is my hobby.*

**A. Underline the finite verbs and circle the non-finite verbs in these sentences.**

1. We watched the clown performing at the circus.
2. It is fun listening to stories from grandparents.
3. The key to achieve success in any task is hard work.
4. He loves to watch birds.
5. How I love walking in the rain!
6. The children displayed the various types of leaves collected by them.
7. The police recovered all the stolen jewellery.
8. The dog began to bark in joy when he saw his master.

## Infinitives, Participles and Gerunds

- The **infinitive** is the base form of a verb. It is usually preceded by *to*. It often functions as a noun in a sentence, acting as the subject or object. For example:

  *He loves to play football.*
  *Vinod and Saurav had gone to watch the movie last night.*

- An infinitive without the preceding *to* is called a **bare infinitive**. For example:

  *I made him help me.*

- **Participles** are words that are used as adjectives. They qualify the nouns that follow them. They can be present, past or perfect participles. For example:

  *Don't try to get up on a running bus. (present participle)*
  *The tired child had fallen asleep immediately. (past participle)*
  *Having finished our lunch, we cleared away the plates. (perfect participle)*

- **Gerunds** are words that look like verbs but function like nouns. They function as the subject of a sentence or the object of a verb or a preposition. For example:

  *He is curious about knowing the result of the competition.*
  *Singing songs makes her happy.*

**B. Fill in the blanks with suitable infinitives.**

*to look*    *to wake*    *to act*    *to help*    *to teach*    *to obey*    *to speak*

1. The teacher tried .......................................... the boy ..........................................
2. He refused .......................................... the truth.
3. They promised .......................................... after the stray puppy.
4. It was kind of you .......................................... the poor boy.
5. It is the duty of every child .......................................... his or her parents.
6. My mother's habit is .......................................... up early in the morning.

**C. Form gerunds from the given options and then fill in the blanks correctly.**

*complete*    *bake*    *eat*    *garden*    *witness*    *win*    *laugh*    *cheat*

1. His favourite pastime is ..........................................; he has grown some rare flowers too.
2. Ravi is confident of .......................................... the match.
3. I managed .......................................... my science project on time.
4. .......................................... relieves a lot of stress.
5. The student was punished for .......................................... in the test.
6. .......................................... the Taj Mahal on a moonlit night was the best part of my trip.
7. Ritu loves .......................................... cakes and cookies.
8. .......................................... ice cream on a hot summer day fills me with joy.

**D. Join the pairs of sentences using participles. One has been done for you.**

1. The baby was crying. The mother tried to calm him.
   The mother tried to calm the crying baby.
2. I finished my work. I went out to play.
   ..........
3. It was a rainy day. I did not venture out.
   ..........
4. Amita found her pen. She had lost it.
   ..........
5. I was fascinated by the book. I bought it.
   ..........
6. He had left home years ago. He had forgotten how his town looked.
   ..........

# LISTENING AND SPEAKING

## Listening

**Listen to the passage and make brief notes under the headings and subheadings.**

Name: ..........

Known for: ..........

..........

Signature look: a. ..........

b. ..........

Events during debut on stage:

a. ..........

..........

b. ..........

..........

c. ..........

..........

d. ..........

..........

e. ..........

..........

# WRITING

## Summary

- A **summary** is the summing up of the main points from a longer passage, yet retaining the essence of the extract.
- You should keep these points in mind:
  - Read the passage carefully and try to reduce the length of the passage to one-third of the original.
  - Mark, underline or make note of the main points. Leave out examples, illustrations and long explanations.
  - Write the summary in your own words, in third person, using phrases from the text only occasionally.
  - Provide a suitable title to the summary.
  - Use impersonal language and neutral tone. Do not add any point of your own.

**Write a summary of the first five paragraphs from the Reading passage about Caesar the crow.**

# 8 Fourteen - II

## READING

**Read this poem about a pair of twins.**

### The Twins

In form and feature, face and limb,
I grew so like my brother,
That folks got taking me for him,
And each for one another.
It puzzled all our kith and kin,
It reached a fearful pitch;
For one of us was born a twin,
Yet not a soul knew which.

One day, to make the matter worse,
Before our names were fixed,
As we were being washed by nurse,
We got completely mixed;
And thus, you see, by fate's decree,
Or rather nurse's whim,
My brother John got christened me,
And I got christened him.

This fatal likeness even dogged
My footsteps when at school,
And I was always getting flogged,
For John turned out a fool.
I put this question, fruitlessly,
To everyone I knew,
'What would you do, if you were me,
To prove that you were you?'

Our close resemblance turned the tide
Of my domestic life,
For, somehow my intended bride
Became my brother's wife.
In fact, year after year, the same
Absurd mistakes went on,
And when I died, the neighbours came
And buried brother John.

*– Henry Sambrooke Leigh*

## COMPREHENSION

**A. Read the lines from the poem and answer the questions.**

1. *It puzzled all our kith and kin...*
   a. What does the phrase 'kith and kin' mean?
   ..................................................
   b. What puzzled the 'kith and kin'? Why were they puzzled?
   ..................................................
   c. Who was responsible for the twins' mix-up?
   ..................................................
2. *This fatal likeness even dogged my footsteps...*
   a. Why is the likeness described as 'fatal'?
   ..................................................
   b. What do you think the poet refers to by the phrase 'dogged my footsteps'?
   ..................................................
   c. How did the footsteps dog the poet in school?
   ..................................................
3. *...turned the tide*
   *Of my domestic life...*
   a. What is meant by the phrase 'turned the tide'?
   ..................................................
   b. How was the tide 'turned'?
   ..................................................
   c. Why did this happen?
   ..................................................

**B. Answer these questions in brief.**

1. How did the twins fare in their studies?

   ..........

   ..........

2. What did the poet ask everyone desperately?

   ..........

   ..........

3. How long did the mistakes in identifying the twins continue?

   ..........

   ..........

4. Between the twins, who had died and what happened then?

   ..........

   ..........

5. Consult a dictionary and write the difference between these two phrases, in the context of the poem.

   a. *fate's decree:*

   ..........

   b. *nurse's whim:*

   ..........

**C. Think and answer these questions.**

1. Who among the twins do you think suffered more for the mistaken identities?

   ..........

   ..........

   ..........

2. Whose life was the poet leading, his or John's?

   ..........

   ..........

   ..........

3. What else do you think could have happened because of the twins' mistaken identities?

   ..........

   ..........

   ..........

# VOCABULARY

## Expressions with *make*

The words *make* and *made*, when combined with some other word or phrase, take on a different meaning. For example:

*make a killing: to make a lot of money very quickly*
*make one's head spin: to confuse someone*
*make light of something: to treat something as unimportant*
*make up: to resolve differences*

**A. Read these sentences that have used different expressions with *make* and *made*. Complete them with the help of the meanings given in the brackets.**

1. I hope I can *make it to* ..........................................; I have been planning for it since ages. (to attend something)
2. The metro officials *made headway* on the .......................................... . (to complete)
3. The .......................................... are continuously *making rounds* .......................................... . (to go from place to place)
4. The .......................................... is *making my mouth water*. (something delicious to eat)
5. .......................................... *makes my blood boil*. (to be extremely angry)
6. .......................................... cannot *make up his mind* about .......................................... . (to decide something)
7. We have to *make do with* .......................................... because I forgot .......................................... . (to manage with what is available)
8. It *made my day* when .......................................... . (made one very happy)

## Commonly Confused Spellings

- English is spoken both in Britain and America with different pronunciations and spellings.
- Look at this table:

| Example | British | American |
|---|---|---|
| humour/humor | *-our* | *-or* |
| centre/center | *-re* | *-er* |
| defence/defense | *-ce* | *-se* |
| catalogue/catalog | *-gue* | *-g* |
| travelling/traveling | *-ll* | *-l* |

**B. Circle the words with British spelling and underline those with American spelling.**

1. apologize
2. color
3. dialog
4. favourite
5. fibre
6. fuelling
7. grey
8. labour
9. license
10. program
11. theatre
12. woollen

## Imagery

- The term **imagery** comes from the word *image* which means *picture*.
- It is used to create a visual or sensory effect by using certain words. For example:

  *lush green stretches*   *soft as a baby's cheeks*

  *fragrant garden*   *spicy tangy food*

**C. Describe the following using suitable imagery of your own.**

1. rain: ..........
2. a tree: ..........
3. a baby: ..........
4. the wind: ..........
5. your mother: ..........
6. night before an exam: ..........
7. smell of your favourite food: ..........
8. a scene that you remember: ..........
   ..........
9. when you got lost for some time, in a crowded place: ..........
   ..........
10. when you first saw a snow-capped mountain peak: ..........
    ..........

# GRAMMAR

## Direct and Indirect Speech

- When we refer to the exact words of the speaker in a sentence, it is said to be in **direct speech**. For example:

  *The narrator asked, 'What would you do, if you were me...?'*

- When we report what somebody said or thought in our own words, we use **indirect speech**. For example:

  *The narrator asked what we would do if we were him.*

A. **Rewrite these sentences in indirect speech. One has been done for you.**

1. 'We will be working in the laboratory all day long,' said the students.
   The students said that they would be working in the laboratory all day long.
2. The teacher said, 'Don't make so much noise!'
3. The librarian said to the members, 'Please return your books before the due date.'
4. The boy said, 'My father has been transferred to Mumbai.'
5. The little girl exclaimed, 'I love comics about superheroes!'
6. Prema said, 'I am reading the latest *Harry Potter* book.'
7. The director said, 'I have been shooting this film for the last two months.'
8. 'We were trapped inside the deep forest,' said the hiker.
9. 'Every action has an equal and opposite reaction,' explained the science teacher.
10. 'I can hear the wind blowing hard,' said the captain of the ship.

## Reporting Verbs

- **Reporting verbs** convey the action of speaking and are used with both direct and indirect speech. Keep these points in mind:
  - They occur after words like *if, whether,* and *that.*
  - They occur after infinitives in the reported speech for commands and requests.
  - They never change when universal truths are talked about in reported speech.
- Some common reporting verbs are *told, asked, ordered, warned, requested, advised, suggested, reminded, exclaimed, cried, apologised, wished,* and *thanked.*

**B. Use suitable reporting verbs and rewrite the sentences in indirect speech.**

1. The robber said to the cashier, 'Don't move!'

2. Surabhi said, 'What a lovely dress mother is wearing!'

3. 'Are you going to Dehradun for the summer vacation?' the child asked her friend.

4. 'Please give me a glass of water,' said the thirsty beggar.

5. 'You should return home before it gets too dark,' Vineet told Sumit.

6. 'What a glorious sunset!' said the tourist in wonder.

7. 'Bird-watching is an unusual hobby that requires tremendous patience,' said the ornithologist.

8. The invigilator said to the examinee, 'Concentrate on your work.'

## LISTENING AND SPEAKING

### Speaking

#### Persuading Someone

- **Persuasive language** is used when we want someone to see our point of view or agree to something we want.

- We use these expressions for persuasion:
    - *What you say is fine, but I think it would be better if…*
    - *We need this immediately, and it cannot be postponed…*
    - *I hope you understand that it must be done now…*
    - *Actually, I think it would be a marvellous idea…*
    - *I'm sure you will see my view…*
    - *I can assure you that…*

**A. Work in pairs and hold conversations on the following topics with your partner. Take turns to role play and try to persuade your partner to agree with you, using suitable language.**

1. your brother to buy something for you
2. your friend to accompany you on a trip to the zoo
3. your father to plan a trip to a hill station
4. your elder sister to give you a treat
5. your mother to hold a party for your birthday
6. your father/mother to allow you to go on a school excursion

## Pronunciation

### Syllables

- A **syllable** is the shortest unit of sound.
- A vowel sound can form a syllable by itself, but a consonant sound always needs a vowel to form a syllable.
- An oblique (/) is often used to mark syllable break in a word. For example:

  2 syllables: *a/gain*    *bas/ket*    *love/ly*    *be/cause*    *in/crease*
  3 syllables: *won/der/ful*    *bi/cy/cle*    *si/lent/ly*    *com/pan/ion*

**B. Break these words into syllables and write the number of syllables in each word.**

1. another ..................................................
2. completely ..................................................
3. domestic ..................................................
4. fearful ..................................................
5. fruitlessly ..................................................
6. intended ..................................................
7. likeness ..................................................
8. mistakes ..................................................

## Word Stress

- Each word can have one syllable stressed for correct pronunciation and articulation.
- Here are some rules that you should follow:
  - In case of nouns, adverbs, and adjectives with two syllables, the stress is on the first syllable. For example:

    *advice, again, pretty, clever, table, council*
  - For verbs with two syllables, the stress is on the last syllable. For example:

    *reject, depend, contrast, figure*
  - For three-syllable words ending in *-er* or *-ly*, the stress is on the first syllable. For example:

    *perfectly, speedily, wearily, manager, caterer*
  - For words ending in *-ic*, *-sion* and *-tion*, the stress is on the second last syllable. For example:

    *decision, dramatic, assumption*

**C. Mention the stressed syllable and the part of speech for each of the words in the given table.**

| Word | Stressed syllable | Part of speech |
|---|---|---|
| 1. adjust | | |
| 2. honest | | |
| 3. counsel | | |
| 4. compare | | |
| 5. lazily | | |
| 6. discuss | | |
| 7. elegant | | |
| 8. artistic | | |
| 9. deception | | |
| 10. seldom | | |

# WRITING

## Short Story

- A **short story** is a brief imaginary tale centred on an incident.
- There is a build-up of incidents which leads to a climax, or the high point of the story, followed by the resolution.

**Write short stories illustrating these proverbs.**

1. *Look before you leap*

2. *Fortune favours the bold*

# TEST 3

(20 marks)

## VOCABULARY ..................................................(5)

**Write the appropriate words for these descriptions.**

1. An expression of exaggeration to say that one cried a lot ..............................
2. An image describing an old house ..............................
3. A word meaning entitlement of rights and correct ..............................
4. An expression using make to mean to feel very happy ..............................
5. Words meaning single and borrowing something ..............................

## GRAMMAR ..................................................(10)

**A. Join the sentences with non-finite verbs and rewrite as stated in the brackets below.** **(3)**

1. Advertising is used for any product. Advertising gives knowledge about the product. (Use infinitive)

   ..............................................................................................................

2. We mostly stay indoors. We are bored of it. (Use gerund)

   ..............................................................................................................

3. I can see a monkey. It is climbing up the tree next to my window. (Use participle)

   ..............................................................................................................

**B. Choose the correct word to fill in the blanks.** **(3)**

1. The scientist asserts that the breaking of a mirror brings misfortune .............................. (is/was) a superstition.
2. Rajam declared that he .............................. (would/will) like to become a teacher.
3. Mr Holmes asked the frightened lady what .............................. (makes/made) her shiver.

**C. Rewrite the sentences changing to direct or indirect speech as required.** **(4)**

1. The lawyer asked his client if he had told him all the details of the case.

   ..............................................................................................................

2. The volunteer said, 'Please donate for the poor Covid stricken families.'

   ..............................................................................................................

3. Mother explained to her little child, 'The sun always sets in the West.'

..............................................................................................................

4. Looking at the sun rise, the tourist exclaimed, 'What a heavenly sight!'

..............................................................................................................

## WRITING ......................................................................................................(5)

**Write a short story using the following hints and give it a title.**

- A monkey leaps into room in search of food
- A man enters the same room to rob
- Reacts and screams on seeing the monkey
- Appropriate conclusion

..............................................................................................................

..............................................................................................................

..............................................................................................................

..............................................................................................................

..............................................................................................................

..............................................................................................................

..............................................................................................................

..............................................................................................................

..............................................................................................................

..............................................................................................................

..............................................................................................................

..............................................................................................................

..............................................................................................................

..............................................................................................................

..............................................................................................................

..............................................................................................................

..............................................................................................................

..............................................................................................................

..............................................................................................................

..............................................................................................................

..............................................................................................................

# 9 Maryam Mirzakhani: Leading the Way

## READING

**Read this passage on the life and times of Marie Curie.**

### Madame Curie

On 7 November 1867, Marie Sklodowska Curie, who was to create history in the world of science, was born in Warsaw, Poland. Her family was quite poor, and she had five siblings. Both her parents were in the teaching profession and inspired her greatly. Her father, a teacher of physics and maths, held a special place in her heart. As a school girl, she loved studying, unlike her peers. With her razor-sharp brain, she naturally topped her class. However, with the Russian invasion, her family's troubles doubled. Her father lost his job and soon after this, her mother died of tuberculosis, adding to the woes of the family.

Marie continued her studies through all the hardships. But day by day, her anxiety increased as the Russians did not permit women to continue studies after the initial schooling, and very few universities admitted girls in those days.

Both Marie and her sister Bonya were passionate about continuing their studies. Their dream was to study in the prestigious Sorbonne University, which was one of the few places to accept girls. But how could they afford the enormous expenses of tuitions, staying in Paris, and travelling! So the sisters made a pact between themselves that while Bonya continued her studies, Marie would support her by working, and then Bonya would do the same for Marie. Bonya studied for six years to graduate as a doctor while Marie worked as a governess, studied math and physics, availing of free courses at an underground university.

Later in 1891, while studying in the Sorbonne, Marie met Pierre Curie, whom she later married. She suffered ill health often, unable to afford staying in heated rooms. However, her brilliant mind ensured that she gained a Master's degree in both physics and chemistry.

Marie was interested in the ongoing researches conducted by Henri Becquerel and Wilhelm Roentgen and their findings about the strength of x-rays and uranium. She too plunged into experiments and finally came up with the theory of radioactivity which stated that an atom could be split, contrary to previous beliefs. As recognition for her work, Marie, along with Henri Becquerel and her husband Pierre Curie were jointly awarded the Nobel in Physics in 1903. In 1911, she discovered polonium and radium, for which she was awarded the Nobel for the second time, in Chemistry. This was an unparalleled feat and had been achieved by none before.

During World War I, Marie was moved after seeing the plight of the wounded soldiers who could not be treated due to the scarcity of x-ray machines. With her daughter Irene, she invented the portable x-ray machine to give quick relief to soldiers. She continued with her experiments on radium, concentrating on how to use it in the medical field, especially in the treatment of tumours. Radium being very expensive, she went to the USA for raising funds and also established a radium research centre in her hometown Warsaw. Even today, people are thankful to her for introducing radium for cancer treatment.

A pioneer in her field, Marie was showered with various accolades, like the Davy Medal, the Albert Medal, and so on. She was the first female professor at the University of Paris, the first woman to be recognised by the Pantheon, and she is till date, the only woman to have won two Nobels in two different sciences.

Being a sincere and dedicated scientist, she continued with her experiments and often carried tubes of radium in her coat. This caused overexposure to radium which led to her suffering from aplastic anaemia, a rare disease in which the bone marrow and stem cells become damaged. Marie Curie died in 1934, aged 66. It is said that her research papers had been so exposed to radiation that they had to be shut in special boxes to prevent further contamination to others. Her life is a testimony on how women can cross numerous barriers to achieve success.

## COMPREHENSION

**A. Fill in the blanks with the correct options.**

1. Marie Curie was .......................................... (*Polish/English*).
2. Marie Curie discovered .......................................... (*uranium/polonium*).
3. Both her Nobel prizes were won .......................................... (*after/before*) World War I.
4. Marie Curie felt .......................................... (*sympathy/apathy*) for the soldiers.
5. She was the first female .......................................... (*student/professor*) at the University of Paris.

**B. Answer the questions in brief.**

1. What were the troubles that Marie faced in her childhood after the Russian invasion?

   ................................................................................

   ................................................................................

2. Why was it not possible for women to continue studies after school?

   ................................................................................

   ................................................................................

3. What was the pact made between Marie and her sister?

   ................................................................................

   ................................................................................

4. How did Marie meet her death?

   ................................................................................

   ................................................................................

5. Give an example of how Marie Curie worked on an equal footing with men.

   ................................................................................

   ................................................................................

6. Find the antonyms of the following words in the passage:

   a. joys: ........................................

   b. abundance: ........................................

**C. Think and answer these questions.**

1. What childhood instance states that Marie's brain was razor-sharp?

   ................................................................................

   ................................................................................

   ................................................................................

2. Why do you think the sisters chose Sorbonne University to study in?

   ................................................................................

   ................................................................................

   ................................................................................

3. What impression do you get about Marie Curie's nature from her work during World War I?

   ................................................................................

   ................................................................................

   ................................................................................

4. How was Marie 'a pioneer in her field'? How was she awarded for her work?

.................................................................................................................................

.................................................................................................................................

.................................................................................................................................

## VOCABULARY

### Forming Abstract Nouns

- **Abstract nouns** are formed from adjectives, verbs, and nouns by adding different suffixes such as *-dom, -ness, -ty, -hood, -ship, -nce, -y, -age, -th, -ism, -ice, -ment, -er,* and *-ise*. For example:

  *Marie continued her studies through all the hardships (from the adjective hard).*
  *But day by day, her anxiety (from the adjective anxious) increased.*

- Look at this table to see how abstract nouns are formed.

| From adjectives | From nouns | From verbs |
|---|---|---|
| honest: honesty | child: childhood | attach: attachment |
| free: freedom | slave: slavery | serve: service |
| strong: strength | friend: friendship | laugh: laughter |

**A. Make abstract nouns from these words. Write the part of speech for each word. One has been done for you.**

| Word | Part of Speech | Abstract Noun |
|---|---|---|
| 1. young | *adjective* | *youth* |
| 2. marry | | |
| 3. artist | | |
| 4. happy | | |
| 5. minister | | |
| 6. use | | |
| 7. behave | | |
| 8. know | | |
| 9. appear | | |
| 10. boy | | |

## Gender Words

- **Gender equality** refers to the fact that the different behavioural aspects, aspirations, and needs of women and men should be considered, valued, and favoured equally.
- Certain terms that you should learn in this context are:
  - *childcare*: the care of children, especially while both parents are at work
  - *empowerment*: confidence due to being in control of one's life
  - *feminism*: the belief and aim that women should have the same rights and opportunities as men
  - *gender discrimination*: the unjust treatment of a particular group of people, because of their gender
  - *gender gap*: the difference that separates men and women, in terms of attitudes, opportunities and status
  - *recognition*: public praise and reward for somebody's work or actions

**B. Fill in the blanks with the gender terms you have just learned.**

1. Women are nowadays bridging the .................................... in almost every field of life.
2. We should fight against any instance of .................................... in the society.
3. Women were granted their rights after a struggle. This is referred to as women ..............................
4. Companies provide for .................................... services, for little children to stay, when both their parents go out to work.
5. Women's Day is celebrated on 8 March in .................................... of women's rights.
6. The idea that a woman should have equal rights and opportunities as a man is called ....................................

# GRAMMAR

## Perfect Tenses

- The **present perfect tense** is used to talk about an action completed in the recent past but whose effects still remain. For example:

  *She has finished eating her dinner.*
  *They have stayed in the city for ten years.*

- The **past perfect tense** is used to talk about a past action that was completed before another past action begun. For example:

  *The train had already left when we reached the station.*
  *Rohini said that they had bought a new house.*

- The **future perfect tense** is used to talk about a future activity that will be finished by or before a specific time in the future.

  *I shall have written the letter by tomorrow.*
  *By the time you reach home, the guests will have left.*

**A. Fill in the blanks with the present perfect form of the given verbs.**

1. My father ...................................... (*finish*) reading the newspaper.
2. I ...................................... (*take*) music lessons for two years.
3. The bell ...................................... just ...................................... (*ring*), announcing the end of recess.
4. ...................................... you ...................................... (*see*) my pen anywhere?
5. My mother ...................................... (*write*) this story for the magazine.
6. We ...................................... already ...................................... (*visit*) the museum twice this month.

**B. Fill in the blanks with the past perfect form of the given verbs.**

1. The family ...................................... already ...................................... (*go*) to bed, when their relatives arrived unannounced.
2. Piku ...................................... (*expect*) India to win the match, but they lost by a narrow margin.
3. Our team ...................................... (*practise*) a lot before the competition began.
4. ...................................... the storm ...................................... (*continue*) for the whole night?
5. I ...................................... (*visit*) the dentist yesterday for my toothache.
6. The children ...................................... (*collect*) dry leaves to make bookmarks before they sold them at the exhibition.

**C. Fill in the blanks with the future perfect form of the given verbs.**

1. By tomorrow we ...................................... (*board*) the train to Jaisalmer.
2. The runners ...................................... (*complete*) their races by this evening.
3. The rescue team ...................................... (*reach*) the accident spot by morning.
4. The forest officials ...................................... (*catch*) the tiger cub by tomorrow.
5. You ...................................... (*cook*) all the dishes by the time our guests arrive.

**D. Fill in the blanks with the correct options.**

1. The young lady ...................................... (*will have secured/has secured*) her driving licence by tomorrow.
2. We have to start now. ...................................... you ...................................... (*Have finished/Had finished*) your breakfast?
3. The naughty children ...................................... (*have plucked/had plucked*) a lot of mangoes by the time the gardener spotted them.
4. I shall go on a trip next month. By then, I ...................................... (*shall have completed/have completed*) my science project.
5. When the guests arrived, my aunt ...................................... (*will have finished/had finished*) cooking.

## Prepositions

- **Prepositions** are words placed before a noun or a pronoun.
- They show the relationship of the noun with the other parts of a sentence. For example:

  *He will come on Monday.*
  *The fox jumped over the wall.*
  *I spotted him walking across the street.*

- This table lists some commonly-used prepositions.

| Prepositions of Time | Prepositions of Place | Prepositions of Movement and Direction |
|---|---|---|
| on, at, before, during, in, till, during, from, since, within, throughout, by | at, above, across, over, under, upon, behind, below, inside, about, near, down | at, away, across, in, on, to, towards, up, into, over, off, round, out of, through, beside, among, between |

**E. Fill in the blanks with suitable prepositions and mention their types.**

1. Everyone was quiet .................................... the concert.
2. He started .................................... Delhi yesterday.
3. The frightened child hid .................................... the door of the shed.
4. India gained her freedom .................................... the year 1947.
5. The swimmer dived .................................... the sea to save the drowning man.
6. Having practised .................................... the day, the band was ready for the concert.
7. The thief ran .................................... with all the money.
8. The bird flew .................................... my head.

# LISTENING AND SPEAKING

## Listening

**Listen to the passage carefully and mark the sentences as true (T) or false (F).**

1. We know Malala's name from the television and newspapers. ☐
2. The condition of girls in the Swat Valley was pathetic. ☐
3. The Taliban were quite broad-minded about people's rights. ☐
4. Malala was aware that her life was in danger. ☐
5. Malala's family was responsible for her fearless attitude. ☐
6. Malala was a teenager when she started writing her blog. ☐
7. Malala wrote the blog under her real name. ☐

# WRITING

## Biography

- A **biography** is the story of a person's life. It is based on the real experiences and achievements of a person.
- A biography should include these details about a person.
  - early life
  - family
  - childhood
  - education
  - hobbies/interests
  - profession
  - experiences
  - achievements
  - awards
  - death

**Write biographical sketches on these personalities. Include relevant and interesting details.**

1. M. S. Dhoni, the World Cup winning captain of the Indian cricket team

2. Charlie Chaplin, the famous actor and comedian

# 10 Teachers

## READING

**Read this poem in the words of a girl child.**

### I Remember

I remember
When I started walking,
Your shoulders had stooped down a bit,
I thought it was to hold me from falling,
But it was the burden, wasn't it?

I remember,
When I saw my brothers going to school,
You chided me for asking for a slate,
I thought I'd done something wrong,
I should have known it was my fate.

I remember,
When you gave my brothers more food,
I ate my hunger and slept at night,
Even that couldn't make you happy,
I just could not do anything right.

– *Ashay Abbhi*

## COMPREHENSION

**A. Read the lines from the poem and answer the questions.**

1. *Your shoulders had stooped down a bit...*

   a. Whose shoulders are being referred to?

   ..........................................................................................

   b. Why are the shoulders 'stooped down'?

   ..........................................................................................

   c. What do you think the poet is trying to express here?

   ..........................................................................................

2. *You chided me for asking...*

   a. What is the meant by 'chided'?

   ..........................................................................................

   b. What had the poet asked?

   ..........................................................................................

   c. What feelings resulted because of the chiding?

   ..........................................................................................

**B. Answer these questions in brief.**

1. When did the poet ask for a slate?

   ..........................................................................................

   ..........................................................................................

2. What did the poet do when her brothers were given more food than her?

   ..........................................................................................

   ..........................................................................................

3. Why does the poet feel that she could not do things right?

   ..........................................................................................

   ..........................................................................................

4. What feelings are being shared through the poem? Give reasons for your answer.

   ..........................................................................................

   ..........................................................................................

   ..........................................................................................

**C. Think and answer these questions.**

1. Who do you think is the poet in the poem?

2. Comment on the use of the expression 'ate my hunger'.

3. Why do you think the phrase 'I remember' is repeated?

## VOCABULARY

### Similes and Metaphors

- A **simile** is a figure of speech in which two things are compared to make the description more vivid. For example:

  *Her face turned as red as a tomato.* (She was embarrassed/felt shy.)

- A **metaphor** is an indirect comparison, where *like* and *as* are not used, as in similes. For example:

  *He is a lion.* (He is brave.)
  *The moon is a lantern in the sky.* (The moon has a soft glow that lights up the sky.)

**A. Identify the things that are being compared in each sentence. Then mention if it is a simile or a metaphor.**

1. Alice ran across the lawn as free as a bird.
2. The dark room was a tomb.
3. The children were butterflies fluttering around the field.
4. My life is a dream come true.
5. The sunshine was like a warm blanket on a cold wintry day.
6. The teeth of the crocodile are little white knives.
7. A book is a key that unlocks the imagination of your mind.
8. Her diary was like her best friend.

**B. Identify the metaphors in these sentences and state their meanings. You may take the help of a dictionary.**

1. Mark Antony gave a fiery speech that moved the people.

   ..........................................................................................................

2. The enemy stormed into the castle and imprisoned the king.

   ..........................................................................................................

3. My father is my rock, always supporting me.

   ..........................................................................................................

4. The camel is the ship of the desert.

   ..........................................................................................................

5. He is the pillar of the family.

   ..........................................................................................................

6. The train thundered through the steep mountains.

   ..........................................................................................................

**C. Complete the sentences with suitable similes.**

1. The long flowing hair of the old woman was as white as ................................ .
2. The naughty girl's eyes twinkled like ................................ when she thought of a new mischief.
3. The little dog was so frightened that he stood still as ................................, behind the door.
4. The steps of the dancer were as graceful as ................................ on water.
5. The disciples were so faithful that they followed their leader like ................................ .
6. The rising sun in the horizon appeared like a ................................ of fire.
7. The meat had not been properly cooked and was as tough as ................................ .

## LISTENING AND SPEAKING

### Speaking

#### Congratulating Someone

- When you have done well in something, you have often heard your parents or friends saying 'We're so proud of you!' This is how we congratulate someone on achieving something.
- Expressions that are used in this context:
  - *I heard the good news! I'm so happy for you.*
  - *Your performance was scintillating... You have scaled new heights...*
  - *You have excelled yourself... What a feat!*
  - *It was no mean achievement, you were astounding!*
  - *I admire how you added another feather to your cap.*

**Role-play with your partner on the following topics, using appropriate congratulatory speech.**

1. You have just received the news that your sister has secured a rank in the board exams.
2. Your aunt has joined a famous organisation.
3. Your younger brother has won a state-level swimming competition.

# WRITING

## Notice Writing

- A **notice** is a formal written communication to inform a group of people about an event.
- It is short and contains only the essential details of the event, including
  - the time, date, and venue.
  - the people for whom the information is meant and the person giving the information.

**Write notices on these topics.**

1. You are the cultural secretary of your school. Your school is organising a science fair, in which students can create and exhibit their scientific inventions, including robots and electronic gadgets. Write a notice inviting students to register their names for the fair.
2. You are the Sports Secretary of your school. Write a notice requesting students to attend an inter-school basketball competition to be organised in the playground, and cheer the school team.
3. You are the head boy/head girl of your school. Write a notice inviting students to participate in the Math Olympiad, that is being organised in the school. Include the eligibility criteria and other necessary details.

# TEST 4

(20 marks)

## VOCABULARY ............................................................ (5)

**A. Complete the sentences with similes.** **(2)**

1. We have been working all day. We are extremely tired and could sleep like ..............................
2. She does not want to do any exercise. She is lazy like ..............................

**B. Identify and underline the metaphor. Then, write which two things have been compared.** **(1.5)**

1. Tears streamed down her face.

   ..............................................................................................

2. He cast an icy look at his enemy.

   ..............................................................................................

3. It is a common saying that laughter is the best medicine.

   ..............................................................................................

**C. Choose the correct abstract noun of the words given.** **(1.5)**

1. friendly

   a. friendship b. friend c. befriend

2. patient

   a. patient b. patiently c. patience

3. female

   a. feminism b. feminine c. femininely

## GRAMMAR ............................................................ (5)

**A. Complete the sentences using the Perfect Tense form of the words in brackets.** **(2)**

1. The police .............................. (catch) the culprit yesterday, by following the clues carefully.
2. The bell .............................. (ring) for assembly but Amit still hasn't reached school.
3. I .............................. (complete) reading *Pride and Prejudice* by tomorrow.
4. I .............................. (watch) the waves on the beach from the morning, and it feels so soothing.

**B. These sentences have incorrect prepositions. Write the incorrect and correct words in the given columns.** **(3)**

| | Error | Correct |
|---|---|---|
| 1. The shawl was kept untidily across the chair. | .............. | .............. |
| 2. The courier kept the parcel down the doorstep. | .............. | .............. |
| 3. She was offered a chair to sit in. | .............. | .............. |

## WRITING ........................................ (10)

**You are the Secretary of the book club of your school. A particular publisher is offering the pupils an opportunity to buy their books at a great discount from the stall they will set up at your school. Write a notice for the students announcing it, informing them also about where to find the list of books available, the procedure of payment, the mode of placing orders and when and how the books will be delivered.**

..............................................................................................................................

..............................................................................................................................

..............................................................................................................................

..............................................................................................................................

..............................................................................................................................

..............................................................................................................................

..............................................................................................................................

..............................................................................................................................

..............................................................................................................................

..............................................................................................................................

..............................................................................................................................

..............................................................................................................................

..............................................................................................................................

..............................................................................................................................

..............................................................................................................................

..............................................................................................................................

..............................................................................................................................

..............................................................................................................................

..............................................................................................................................

..............................................................................................................................

# 11 Goodbye, Pasha Begum!

## READING

**Read this passage about how a volcano wiped out two towns.**

### Pompeii

In ancient Rome, two seaside towns, Pompeii and Herculaneum used to be vibrant with life. These towns were situated in the shade of an ominous volcano called Vesuvius. But that did not bother the inhabitants as it had long shown no signs of life. The towns were always bustling with activity. Pompeii was a rich town with people travelling in chariots, and there were crossings for pedestrians too. There were open-air theatres, barracks for gladiators, public baths, and magnificent private homes. The town spoke of the wealth and the artistic sense of its citizens. Gorgeous paintings and portraits decorated the walls of the houses. Ornamental statues adorned the gardens and fountains spewed water majestically.

Unfortunately, this town was silenced forever on 24 August AD 79. On this day, people went about their activities as usual. There was a general excitement in the air with people discussing the upcoming elections. In the port, cargoes were being loaded. It was summer, so a gay, colourful holiday crowd was seen in the markets. People were blissfully unaware of the fearful disaster that was to fall on them. A faint indication of this had happened, seventeen years ago, when an earthquake rocked Pompeii, destroying buildings. But this tremor did not alarm the people.

On that particular morning, after eleven, a thick large cloud, shaped like a mushroom, could be seen covering the sky. Darkness descended, and the day appeared like night. Suddenly hot sparks flew out of the volcano and the air was filled with thick sulphurous fumes. The mighty Vesuvius had erupted. Molten lava spilled out, and the people felt the searing heat enveloping and suffocating them. Terrified, they tried to escape. Some ran to take shelter in the underground cellars but were choked and buried there. Roof tops and upper stories of houses collapsed and caved in. With the first surge, the temperature ranged from 182–220 degrees Celsius. By evening there was nothing left standing. The lava spill continued throughout the second day, burying them under two metres deep ash. By the third day, these places had been transformed from seaside towns to plain stretches of nothingness.

With the passing of centuries, the towns went into oblivion. However, one day in the middle of the eighteenth century, a farmer, ploughing the ground for his vineyard, suddenly struck upon something hard. Experts were informed and the ruins of these towns were discovered. After a long-drawn process of excavation, an entire picture of ancient Roman life emerged, complete, with not only the public notices and sales announcements on walls, but also with its pottery, jewellery, and even a table set for a meal!

## COMPREHENSION

**A. Fill in the blanks with the correct options.**

1. Vesuvius had been .................................... (*a dormant/an active*) volcano.
2. People were .................................... (*conscious/casual*) about the presence of a volcano nearby.
3. The volcano erupted in the .................................... (*morning/night*).
4. The lava spill continued for .................................... (*two/three*) days.
5. The discovery of the ruins was .................................... (*accidental/planned*).

**B. Answer the questions in brief.**

1. How is it apparent that Pompeii was a rich town?

   ....................................................................................................

   ....................................................................................................

2. Why were the people excited on the day of the eruption?

   ....................................................................................................

   ....................................................................................................

3. How did the weather change that fateful day?

   ....................................................................................................

   ....................................................................................................

4. What happened to the houses during the eruption?

   ....................................................................................................

   ....................................................................................................

5. Why could the people of the towns not escape?

   ....................................................................................................

   ....................................................................................................

6. Write down the meanings of the following:

   a. spewed: ..........................................  c. searing: ..........................................

   b. blotted out: ..........................................  d. excavation: ..........................................

**C. Think and answer the questions.**

1. How do you know that Pompeii was a seaside town?

   ..........................................................................................................

   ..........................................................................................................

   ..........................................................................................................

2. What indication do you get of the fact that the eruption was totally unexpected?

   ..........................................................................................................

   ..........................................................................................................

   ..........................................................................................................

3. What do you think the expression 'the towns went into oblivion' means?

   ..........................................................................................................

   ..........................................................................................................

   ..........................................................................................................

4. What message about nature does the passage imply? Explain your answer.

   ..........................................................................................................

   ..........................................................................................................

   ..........................................................................................................

# VOCABULARY

## Collocations

- **Collocations** are words that are usually spoken or written together in English language. For example:

  *big surprise*  *resounding success*

- These can be of the following types:
  - adjective and noun: *big deal*
  - verb and noun: *commit crime*
  - verb and preposition: *depend on*
  - verb and adverb: *sob hysterically*

**A. Fill in the blanks with the correct options. One has been done for you.**

1. The old man ..gave.. (*gave/told*) advice to his grandson.
2. The student came ................................ (*ready/prepared*) for the examination.

3. The little boy ................................ (*does/makes*) his bed every day.
4. He has a ................................ (*great/big*) admiration for his hero.
5. The vendor bought a ................................ (*large/heavy*) quantity of fruits to sell.
6. The child was absent ................................ (*from/at*) school yesterday.
7. The lawyer put forth a ................................ (*great/strong*) argument to fight his case.
8. The survivor of the crash recounted his experience in ................................ (*large/great*) details.

**B. Combine the words of Column A with those of Column B to make collocations.**

| Column A | Column B | Collocation |
|---|---|---|
| 1. bygone | a. affinity | |
| 2. foul | b. diet | |
| 3. heavy | c. era | |
| 4. nourishing | d. joke | |
| 5. practical | e. order | |
| 6. strong | f. smell | |
| 7. tall | g. traffic | |

## Proverbs

**Proverbs** are well-known phrases or sentences that give advice or say something that is generally true. For example:

*Where there is a will there is a way.*
(When you are determined to do something, you will find a way to do it.)
*Rome was not built in a day.*
(Every good thing takes time to finish.)
*Actions speak louder than words.*
(You are judged by what you do rather than what you say.)

**C. There are often two proverbs with the same meaning. Find out what the meaning might be. You can use a dictionary. One has been done for you.**

1. Better safe than sorry./Prevention is better than cure.
   It is wiser to be too careful than to act too quickly.
2. All that glitters is not gold./Don't judge a book by its cover.
   ................................................................................
3. Once bitten, twice shy./A burnt child dreads the fire.
   ................................................................................

4. Birds of a feather flock together./A man is known by the company he keeps.

..........................................................................................

5. The early bird catches the worm./First come, first served.

..........................................................................................

6. As you sow, so you shall reap./As man lives, so shall he die.

..........................................................................................

7. Don't count your chickens before they are hatched./Don't cross a bridge until you come to it.

..........................................................................................

8. Make hay while the sun shines./Strike while the iron is hot.

..........................................................................................

## DICTIONARY SKILLS

### Derivatives

- **Derivatives** are words which are formed from the base or the root word.
- They are formed by adding either prefixes before or suffixes after the root word.
- Look at this table below.

| Base word | Derivatives |
|---|---|
| base | basic, basically |
| central | centralize, centrally |
| humour | humorous, humorously |
| kind | kindness, kindly |
| discipline | disciplinary |
| emphasis | emphasize, emphatic, emphatically |
| sense | sensibility, sensible, sensibly |
| educate | education, educational |

**A. Form new derivatives from these words.**

1. audio: ..........................................................
2. enter: ..........................................................
3. friend: ..........................................................
4. grammar: ..........................................................

5. fool: ..........

6. honour: ..........

7. labour: ..........

8. occur: ..........

9. origin: ..........

10. simple: ..........

11. touch: ..........

**B. Add prefixes to these words to make derivatives.**

1. break: .......... 6. legal: ..........
2. circle: .......... 7. locate: ..........
3. control: .......... 8. number: ..........
4. courage: .......... 9. valuable: ..........
5. friend: .......... 10. warn: ..........

**C. Add suffixes to these words to form derivatives.**

1. absent: .......... 6 globe: ..........
2. book: .......... 7. moment: ..........
3. character: .......... 8. nation: ..........
4. just: .......... 9. picture: ..........
5. king: .......... 10. water: ..........

# GRAMMAR

## Simple, Complex, and Compound Sentences

- A **simple sentence** contains only one finite verb and one independent clause. For example:

  *I had mango juice now.*
  *Vani and her sister sent me a birthday card.*

- A **compound sentence** contains at least two independent clauses. These clauses are joined by a coordinating conjunction or a semicolon. For example:

  *Shireen went to the market and bought some vegetables.*
  *The dancers lined up; the show began.*

- A **complex sentence** contains one main clause and one or more subordinate clauses. The clauses are joined using subordinate conjunctions or relative pronouns. For example:

  *If everyone is present, we will start the session.*
  *Alice went through the door which was red in colour.*

**A. Identify if these sentences are simple (S), compound (CO) or complex (C).**

1. On reaching school, we will meet the principal. ☐
2. He is not only a tennis player, but also a long-distance runner. ☐
3. Man is the architect of his own fortune. ☐
4. Always remember that every person should be respected. ☐
5. He is poor yet content with his lot. ☐
6. You must work hard if you want success. ☐
7. The stranger whom I met yesterday is an Englishman. ☐
8. During the lunch break, the children rushed out to play. ☐
9. Study hard or you will fail. ☐
10. Hill stations are my favourite places to visit. ☐

**B. Complete these sentences and state whether they are simple, complex, or compound.**

1. A healthy man is one who ..................................................................
2. I am an old coin, and I ..................................................................
3. .................................................................. is my favourite food.
4. Last night, I heard footsteps behind me when ..................................................................
5. Fast food is tasty but it ..................................................................
6. The importance of the newspaper has not lessened though ..................................................................
7. Do not neglect your studies or ..................................................................
8. I like reading the *Percy Jackson* books because ..................................................................
9. .................................................................. play an important part in our lives.
10. You will be thoroughly drenched in the rain if ..................................................................

## Punctuation

### Semicolon and Colon

- A **semicolon** (;) is a longer pause than a comma but a shorter pause than a full stop.
- It connects two separate sentences together instead of a conjunction. For example:

  *The boys planned a picnic. They are excited.*
  *The boys planned a picnic; they are excited.*

- A **colon** (:) is a longer pause than a semicolon but a shorter pause than a full stop.
- It acts as a pause which introduces related information. For example:

  *That is the good thing about Tanya: she always owns up her mistake and is forgiven soon.*

  *There are many places of tourist interest in Hyderabad: the Golconda Fort, the Salar Jung Museum, and Ramoji Film City.*

**C. Punctuate these sentences with semicolon and colon.**

1. The boy fell sick he was not chosen for the play.
2. Do advise me which stream to choose medical or engineering.
3. I have read an essay entitled *William Shakespeare His Life and His Plays.*
4. He was going on a vacation he was excited.
5. Here is what you need to get from the market a loaf of bread, a packet of cheese, and a dozen bananas.
6. I would love to join you all for the trek my health would not permit.

# LISTENING AND SPEAKING

## Listening

**A. Listen to the passage carefully. Complete the sentences with the correct information.**

1. The Easter Island was discovered in the .............................................. century.
2. The statues had no .............................................. .
3. The statues were made of .............................................. and weighed up to .............................................. .
4. Some people consider the island to be a .............................................. for the nearby islands that have disappeared due to .............................................. .
5. The second theory about the origin of the island states that .............................................. who were strong enough to .............................................. .
6. 'Others' is the name of .............................................. .
7. The third theory states that the Easter Island was once part of a .............................................., and the statues were worshipped as .............................................. .

## Speaking

### Reader's Theatre

- **Reader's theatre** is a style of theatre in which the actors do not memorise their lines. Instead, they read their respective lines out from a script.
- The actors use only vocal modulations to convey feelings and actions, rather than using elaborate sets and costumes.

**B. Take the Reading Comprehension from Chapter 7 of this book. Write a script on what the dialogues might be in the context of Caesar the crow's naughty behaviour. Divide the text into five scenes. Choose characters, even one person can play multiple roles. Read the script silently at first to get an idea about it and underline the key words and important expressions. Stand or sit in a semicircle, and use only voice modulations to indicate your role.**

The five scenes can be:

Scene 1: Discovery of the wounded crow by the boy and his grandfather—decision to take it home

Scene 2: Reaction of grandmother—care taken of the crow and name given to it

Scene 3: Caesar's behaviour on the dining table—grandmother's comments

Scene 4: Caesar's naughty deeds and the reaction of the family

Scene 5: Neighbours complaining about Caesar and how the family deals with them

## Pronunciation

### Sentence Stress

- While speaking, we stress on the important words in a sentence to convey the message clearly.
- Usually the content or key words are stressed on, and not the other structure words of the sentence.

Read the sentences, stressing the highlighted words and note how the meaning changes.

*How I* **love** *walking in the rain.*
**How** *I love walking in the rain.*
*How I love* **walking** *in the rain.*
*How I love walking in the* **rain**.

**C. Read this poem by Lewis Carroll from *Alice in Wonderland*. Stress on the words in italics and not on the underlined words.**

How <u>doth</u> <u>the</u> little *crocodile*
*Improve* <u>his</u> shining tail,
<u>And</u> pour the *waters* <u>of</u> the Nile
<u>On</u> every *golden* scale!

How *cheerfully* he seems <u>to</u> grin.
How *neatly* spreads his claws,
And *welcomes* little fishes <u>in</u>
<u>With</u> *gently* smiling jaws!

# WRITING

## Making a Travel Brochure

- A **travel brochure** is a small magazine or a book containing pictures and information about a place or advertising the special points of a trip.
- It helps us prepare our schedule beforehand and plan our trip accordingly. For making such a brochure, note these points.
  - The heading should be attractive.
  - Pictures of monuments or places of renown should be used.
  - One can experiment with the font style.
  - Legends, origin, architectural history of the place to be stated.
  - Nearby sightseeing places to be mentioned.
  - Details about hotels and available transportation to be given.
  - Attractive packages to be mentioned, along with discounts, if any.

**Prepare a travel brochure on your favourite place to visit. It can be a hill station, historical city, beach resort, or a desert town. Remember to highlight all the points that make this place so special to you.**

# 12 Try Again

## VOCABULARY

### Archaic Words

- **Archaic words** are old English words that are no longer used.
- They are a part of ancient literature and add colour and character to language, even today. For example:

  *asunder: apart* — *avaunt: go away*
  *dame: an elderly woman* — *forsooth: indeed*

**Identify the archaic words in the sentences. Then match the words with their meanings, given in the box.**

| *gossiping* | *attacked* | *look* | *plead* | *wonderful and extraordinary* | *tangled and messy hair* | *arguing* | *in a little while* |
|---|---|---|---|---|---|---|---|

1. Behold, here comes King Richard. ..........................
2. Stop twattling, and get back to work. ..........................
3. Have you seen the state of my elflocks today? ..........................
4. The movie was as monsterful as the advertisements and trailers stated. ..........................
5. The two sisters were brabbling over who will do the chores. ..........................
6. I hear you calling and I will come anon. ..........................
7. I beseech you; have mercy. ..........................
8. The politician was bombarded with questions from the press. ..........................

# WRITING

## Writing Tweets

- **Tweets** are short messages written online on the social networking site called *Twitter*.
- Keep these points in mind while tweeting.
  - Tweets are written in a conversational style.
  - Words as *see, look, you, follow,* and *check out* are used quite often.
  - Tweets convey a sense of urgency. They may be brief, but contain the message that needs to be passed.
  - A tweet can have 280 characters generally, except in a few languages.

**Read this sample Twitter conversation below.**

**You are working on a project on *Ancient Empires of the World*. Discuss this with your friend through tweets.**

Amal: Hey, working on the project. Need help.

Biswajit: Sure, which empire are you working on: Egypt or Greece? How can I help?

Amal: Trying to cover the Roman Empire. Want information about when it was formed and under whom.

Biswajit: In 31 BC, under Caesar Augustus who brought peace, prosperity, and culture.

Amal: Thanks. Curious to note how such a vast empire could fall due to German attacks in AD 476. Done with your project?

Biswajit: Actually, having a bit of a problem regarding the location of the Mayan and Inca Empire.

Amal: Father told me that the Mayan Empire was spread across southern Mexico and northern central America.

Amal: The Inca Empire was spread over South America, including Columbia, Bolivia, and Argentina.

Biswajit: Thanks, that was a great help.

Amal: Thanks to you too. Bye then, back to work now. Will talk after the Arsenal vs Manchester United match.

Biswajit: I'm sure Arsenal will win. Anyway, more after the match!

**Now tweet to your friend, exchanging views about a recent movie that you enjoyed.**

# TEST 5

(20 marks)

## VOCABULARY ........................................ (5)

**Pair the words with their correct meanings. Then, write the answers in the blanks provided.**

| | | |
|---|---|---|
| 1. ere (modern form) | now<br>before<br>after | .................................... |
| 2. make (collocation) | a home<br>trouble<br>shift | .................................... |
| 3. malice seldom (proverb) | turns chance into good fortune<br>cast their shadows before<br>wants a mark to shoot at | .................................... |
| 4. betwixt (modern form) | between<br>among<br>various | .................................... |
| 5. accept (derivative) | exceptional<br>acceptable<br>acceptional | .................................... |

## GRAMMAR ........................................ (10)

**A. Complete the following sentences. Then, write if they are Simple, Compound or Complex sentences in the brackets.** **(4)**

1. *The Tale of Two Cities* is a novel which ....................................

   ( .................................... )

2. We cannot fly a kite unless....................................

   ( .................................... )

3. I not only bought a new dress ..........................................................................................

   ( .............................................. )

4. The family living on the floor above us ...............................................................................

   ( .............................................. )

**B. The meanings of some proverbs contrast each other. Here are some examples of such proverbs. Match the opposite pairs.** **(3)**

| | |
|---|---|
| 1. Absence makes the heart go fonder. | a. The pen is mightier than the sword. |
| 2. Two heads are better than one. | b. Out of sight out of mind |
| 3. Actions speak louder than words. | c. Too many cooks spoil the broth. |

**C. Punctuate the sentences with colon or semi colon wherever required.** **(3)**

1. I have read an interesting book *Martian Chronicles* by Ray Bradbury.
2. The child asked for three things to paint water colours, paint brush and a palette.
3. The police announced this it is unsafe to step outside during the lockdown as the risk of infection increases.

## WRITING ..........................................................................................................(5)

**A. Make a travel brochure on a historical site that you have visited.** **(3)**

**B. Write a tweet expressing your views on the poor drainage conditions in a slum that you visited. Remember to keep your message within 280 words.** **(2)**

# 13 The Diary of a Space Traveller

## READING

**Read this passage about the adventures of an invisible man.**

### The Invisible Man

Suddenly the stranger raised his clenched gloved hand, stamped his foot and said, 'Stop!' with extraordinary violence.

'You don't understand,' he said, 'who I am or what I am. I'll show you. By Heaven, I'll show you.' Then he put his open palm over his face and withdrew it. The centre of his face became a black cavity.

'Here,' he said. He stepped forward and handed Mrs Hall something. The lady was too stunned and accepted it automatically. When she saw what it was, she screamed loudly, dropped it and staggered back. A nose— it was the stranger's pink nose! Pink and shining— it rolled on the floor.

Then he removed his spectacles, and everyone gasped. He took off his hat, and with a violent gesture, tore at the whiskers and bandages that acted as his face. For a moment, they resisted him.

'Oh my God!' cried someone. Then they came off.

It was worse than anything. Mrs Hall stood open-mouthed and horror struck, shrieked at what she saw and made for the door of the house. Everyone began to move. They were prepared for scars, disfigurements, horrors that could be seen, but *nothing*! The bandages and false hair flew across the passage making everyone jump in order to avoid them. People tumbled over each other in their rush to get away from him. For the man who stood there shouting, was a solid gesticulating figure up to the coat collar, and then… nothingness! No visible thing at all!

Suddenly, Mr Hall marched up the stairs with the police.

'Constable, do your duty,' he said. They marched in. They saw the headless figure with a gnawed crust of bread in one glove and a chunk of cheese in another.

'That's him!' said Hall.

'What's this?' came an angry tone from above the collar of the figure.

As they advanced, the figure said, 'Keep off!'

The policeman, Jaffers, charged towards the bread and cheese and just grasped the knife.
Off came the left gloves and slapped Jaffers in the face. He then gripped the headless figure by his handless wrist and caught his invisible throat. He got a resounding kick on the shin.
Both swayed, staggered, clutching and hitting at each other.

'I'll surrender,' said the stranger.

Jaffers produced a pair of handcuffs. 'Can't use them as I can see,' he said.

The stranger ran his arm down his waistcoat, and as if by miracle, the buttons to which his empty sleeve pointed came undone. Then he said something about his shin and stooped down. He seemed to be fumbling with his shoes and socks.

'Why!' said one of the men suddenly, 'That's not a man at all. It's just empty clothes. Look! You can see down his collar.'

He extended his hand; it seemed to meet something in mid-air, and he drew back with a sharp exclamation.

'I'd wish you keep your fingers out of my eye,' said an aerial voice, in an angry tone.
'The fact is, I'm all here: head, hands, legs, and all the rest of it, but I happen to be invisible.'

'Invisible?'

'Yes. It's strange, perhaps, but not a crime. Why am I being assaulted by a policeman in this fashion?'

*(Excerpted from 'The Invisible Man' by H. G. Wells)*

## COMPREHENSION

**A. The invisible man had covered himself with various items of clothing. Match the clothing with what it covered.**

| Body part | Clothing |
|---|---|
| 1. nose | a. bandage and whiskers |
| 2. feet | b. trousers |
| 3. hands | c. shoes and socks |
| 4. face | d. false pink cover |
| 5. legs | e. spectacles |
| 6. chest | f. gloves |
| 7. eyes | g. waistcoat |

**B. Answer the questions in brief.**

1. Why did Mrs Hall scream loudly?

..............................................................................

..............................................................................

2. What caused everyone to tumble over each other?

..............................................................................

..............................................................................

3. What did the police see on marching into the room?

..............................................................................

..............................................................................

4. Why could Jaffers not use the handcuffs?

..............................................................................

..............................................................................

5. When the man extended his arm, what did he 'meet mid-air'?

..............................................................................

..............................................................................

6. Write the antonyms of the following.

   a. violence: ..................................  b. shining: ..................................

**C. Think and answer the questions.**

1. Why do you think the man tried to hide his invisibility?

..............................................................................

..............................................................................

..............................................................................

2. Why was the invisible man trying to evade arrest?

..............................................................................................................

..............................................................................................................

..............................................................................................................

3. How was the invisible man at an advantage over the others who tried to capture him?

..............................................................................................................

..............................................................................................................

..............................................................................................................

4. How do you think Jaffers was able to hit the invisible man even though he could not see him?

..............................................................................................................

..............................................................................................................

..............................................................................................................

## VOCABULARY

### Science Fiction Words

- There are many words that we come across specifically when we read science fiction or space adventure stories.
- These are also commonly used in sci-fi movies. For example:

  *alien, ray gun, spaceship, cyberspace, robot, superhero, parallel universe, telepathy, extra-terrestrial, humanoid, fourth dimension, UFO, beam, x-ray vision*

**A. Complete this passage with words from the list given above. The meanings of the words are given in the brackets. One has been done for you.**

An ...extra-terrestrial... (*being from outer space*) from .............................. (*a different space*) in a .............................. (*a universe like ours*) landed on Earth. He descended from the .............................. (*the transport used to travel in space*) and looked around the beautiful green trees. He was impressed and wanted to conquer this world. So, he started to explore the new territory with a .............................. (*a kind of weapon*). Suddenly, he saw an upright figure, wearing a flowing cloak, with a mask on his face.

He thought, 'This must be a .................................. (*a being like humans*) that I have heard of.' He extended his antennae to feel it, when the ..................................(*a being with great powers*) spotted him. Immediately, he looked through him with his ..................................(*something that enables one to see beneath the surface covering*). He concluded that it was an .................................. (*a creature from outer space*) which walked like a ..................................(*a mechanical being*). Also, by using .................................. (*power of reading thoughts*), he realised that this creature had ambitious plans about conquering Earth. He started emitting red-hot .................................. (*rays*) from his eyes to destroy it. The creature felt the burning heat and could not tolerate the searing pain. It quickly ran back to the .................................. (*the vehicle it had travelled in*) and zoomed off in it.

## Same Words used as Different Parts of Speech

Sometimes, a word can be used as different parts of speech, depending on how it is used in a sentence. For example:

*People tumbled over each other. (verb)*
*The jockey took a nasty tumble while trying to clear the fence. (noun)*

*He has chosen the right path. (adjective)*
*Being under 18, you do not have the right to vote yet. (noun)*

**B. State the part of speech for the italicised words in these sentences.**

1. His supporters *back* him in whatever he says or does. ..................................
2. The thief entered through the *back* door. ..................................
3. The new girl was standing in the *last* row. ..................................
4. The provisions of the mountaineers *lasted* for a month. ..................................
5. The police *handed* over the clues to the detective. ..................................
6. The king's brother definitely had a *hand* in the plot to dethrone him. ..................................
7. The examinee put a *tick* for the correct answer. ..................................
8. The hands of the clock *ticked* away. ..................................
9. The dog *bared* its teeth, sensing danger. ..................................
10. The poor little girl walked *bare*-foot. ..................................

**C. Make sentences with the words according to the instructions given in brackets.**

1. air (*noun*): ..................................
   air (*verb*): ..................................
2. close (*verb*): ..................................
   close (*adjective*): ..................................
3. long (*adjective*): ..................................
   long (*verb*): ..................................

4. blame (*noun*): ..................................................

blame (*verb*): ..................................................

5. second (*noun*): ..................................................

second (*adjective*): ..................................................

# GRAMMAR

## Main and Subordinate Clauses

- You know that a **clause** is a group of words that contain a subject and a finite verb.
- Clauses are broadly of two types:
  - A **main clause** has a subject and a finite verb and makes complete sense by itself.
  - A **subordinate clause** has a finite verb and a subject but does not make complete sense on its own. It depends on the main clause for its meaning.
  - In the following sentences, the words in colour form the main clause, while the underlined words form the subordinate clause.

    *Lata likes to eat apple pies* *if they are hot and freshly-baked*.
    *I know the singer* *who performed at the concert last night*.

**A. Underline the main clauses and circle the subordinate clauses in these sentences.**

1. As soon as I got the news, I rushed home.
2. She listened carefully as the teacher read out the text.
3. I finally have the set of watercolours which I had wanted.
4. Please tell me the answer to this question.
5. You are a wonderful friend.
6. The boy ran after the kite.
7. This is the autograph of the author whom I met yesterday.
8. I sent her a birthday card as I was unable to attend her party.
9. The stamp collection which is displayed in the cupboard belongs to my uncle.
10. Priya missed the event because she was down with a fever.

## Relative Clauses

- **Relative clauses** start with the **relative pronouns** *who, that, which, whose, where,* and *when.*
- They are most often used to define or identify the noun that precedes them. For example:

  *The boy who won the competition is his nephew.*
  *The shop where I bought the bangles is right around this corner.*

**B. Join each pair of sentences with suitable relative pronouns.**

1. Many snakes have poisonous fangs. These fangs produce deadly venom.

   ..........................................................................................

2. Akbar had nine clever men in his court. He referred to them as his nine jewels.

   ..........................................................................................

3. Danny's heart was full of joy at his friend's arrival. It was also full of fear for his safety.

   ..........................................................................................

4. Once upon a time, there was a wizard. He used to disguise himself as a beggar.

   ..........................................................................................

5. This is my sister. I always borrow her dresses.

   ..........................................................................................

6. I went to Darjeeling. I boarded the magical toy train there.

   ..........................................................................................

## LISTENING AND SPEAKING

### Listening

**Listen to the passage carefully. Then match the effects with their causes.**

| Effect | Cause |
|---|---|
| 1. The heart has to work harder. | a. These become weak in the absence of gravity, and due to a lack of activity. |
| 2. The astronauts need to exercise the lower parts of their bodies. | b. It would scatter all over the place. |
| 3. They use a special soap. | c. They may suffer injury. |
| 4. Their food is in packets. | d. It has to work against no gravity. |
| 5. They strap themselves to the bed. | e. They have to control the use of water in space. |
| 6. They sleep facing the ventilator. | f. The solid food would not float in the air. |
| 7. Their plates have magnets underneath. | g. They may have breathing trouble. |

## WRITING

### Report Writing

- A **report** is an account of an event that has taken place.
- It has a clear purpose and a specific audience in mind.
- It should have a title, be brief and should convey only the important points in a neutral tone.

**Your school had recently organised a pet adoption drive in collaboration with the local animal rescue shelter. Many students attended it with their parents, and a lot of animals were adopted as well. Write a report about it for your school newsletter or wall magazine.**

# 14 The Quest for Extraterrestrial Life

## READING

**Read the poem about the first journey to the moon made by Neil Armstrong and Buzz Aldrin.**

### First Moon Landing

Two highfliers
Buzz and Neil,
Said they couldn't
Wait to feel
Just what kind of
Moon it was—
'Take a look around'
Said Buzz.

Open the hatch
And out of the door,
Down the ladder
To the moonlit floor.
After he had
Sunk his heel
Into the dusty
Ocean, Neil
Knew what a lovely
Moon it was—
'One small step…'
Said Neil to Buzz.

*– J. Patrick Lewis*

## COMPREHENSION

**A. Read the lines from the poem and answer the questions.**

1. *'Take a look around...'*
   a. Where did the speaker want to 'take a look around'?

   ..........

   b. Why did they want to do so?

   ..........

   c. What were their feelings then?

   ..........

2. *To the moonlit floor...*
   a. What floor is being referred to?

   ..........

   b. How did the speakers reach there?

   ..........

   c. What happens after they step onto the 'moonlit floor'?

   ..........

3. *Said Neil to Buzz.*
   a. Who do you think Neil and Buzz are in the poem?

   ..........

   b. What do you think is their profession?

   ..........

   c. What do they travel in?

   ..........

**B. Answer these questions in brief.**

1. What did Buzz and Neil say at the beginning of the poem?

   ..........

   ..........

2. What do you think is a 'hatch', in the context of this poem?

   ..........

   ..........

3. What is the rhyme scheme used in the poem?

   ..........

   ..........

4. What do you think is the poet referring to by the expression 'dusty ocean'?

   ..........

   ..........

## C. Think and answer these questions.

1. Why do you think Buzz and Neil are called 'highfliers'?

2. What actual event is being spoken about in the poem?

3. Why is the expression 'what kind of moon it was' used?

4. Neil had said 'one small step' at the end of the poem. Can you guess what he might have said next?

# VOCABULARY

## One Word Substitution

- **One word substitution** happens when a single word replaces a group of words or a complete sentence, without changing its meaning.
- This helps in enriching one's vocabulary, making it crisp and concise. For example:

  a person who is unknown: *anonymous*
  things to be done throughout the day: *schedule*
  something that cannot be heard: *inaudible*

**A. Match the words with the group of words they can replace.**

| Group of words | One word |
|---|---|
| 1. something that cannot be read | a. *diplomat* |
| 2. life-story of a man written by himself | b. *incredible* |
| 3. that which occurs once a year | c. *kleptomaniac* |
| 4. something which cannot be believed | d. *psychology* |
| 5. a person who represents the country in a foreign land | e. *anonymous* |
| 6. the study of human behaviour | f. *illegible* |
| 7. one who has a habit of stealing | g. *autobiography* |
| 8. a sweet dish eaten at the end of a meal | h. *annual* |
| 9. the young one of a kangaroo | i. *fugitive* |
| 10. a place where birds are kept | j. *joey* |
| 11. a person who is unknown | k. *aviary* |
| 12. one who is on the run from law | l. *dessert* |

**B. Replace the underlined words in the sentences choosing from the words given.**

*maiden* *illiterate* *illegal* *optimism* *incorrigible* *refugee* *philanthropist* *panacea* *ambidextrous* *numismatist*

1. The condition of a <u>man forced to leave his country and take shelter in another country</u> is uncertain. ......................
2. People who are full of <u>the quality to look at the bright side of things</u> are usually happy. ......................
3. He travels from country to country as he is a <u>person interested in the study of coin, paper money, tokens</u>. ......................
4. He is respected everywhere, as he is a <u>person who helps those in need and donates for charity</u>. ......................
5. The doctor is popular as he seems to have a <u>solution or remedy for all difficult diseases</u>. ......................
6. The government should provide education for the <u>people who cannot read or write</u>. ......................
7. The smuggler has been arrested as his trade is <u>not permitted by law</u>. ......................
8. The teachers have tried to reform his habits, but in vain. He is <u>one who cannot be corrected</u>. ......................
9. After the accident and the resultant physiotherapy sessions, the woman has become <u>capable of using both hands equally well</u>. ......................
10. Though it was the statesman's <u>first occasion</u> speech, it impressed the audience. ......................

## Mind Maps

- A **mind map** is a visual way of representing information, helping in easy recollection of concepts learnt.
- In this diagrammatic form of note taking or note making, the central idea is placed in the middle and associated ideas are arranged around the core concept, in branches that map out.

C. **Use this figure to make a mind map on space expeditions. You can look up information on the Internet for this.**

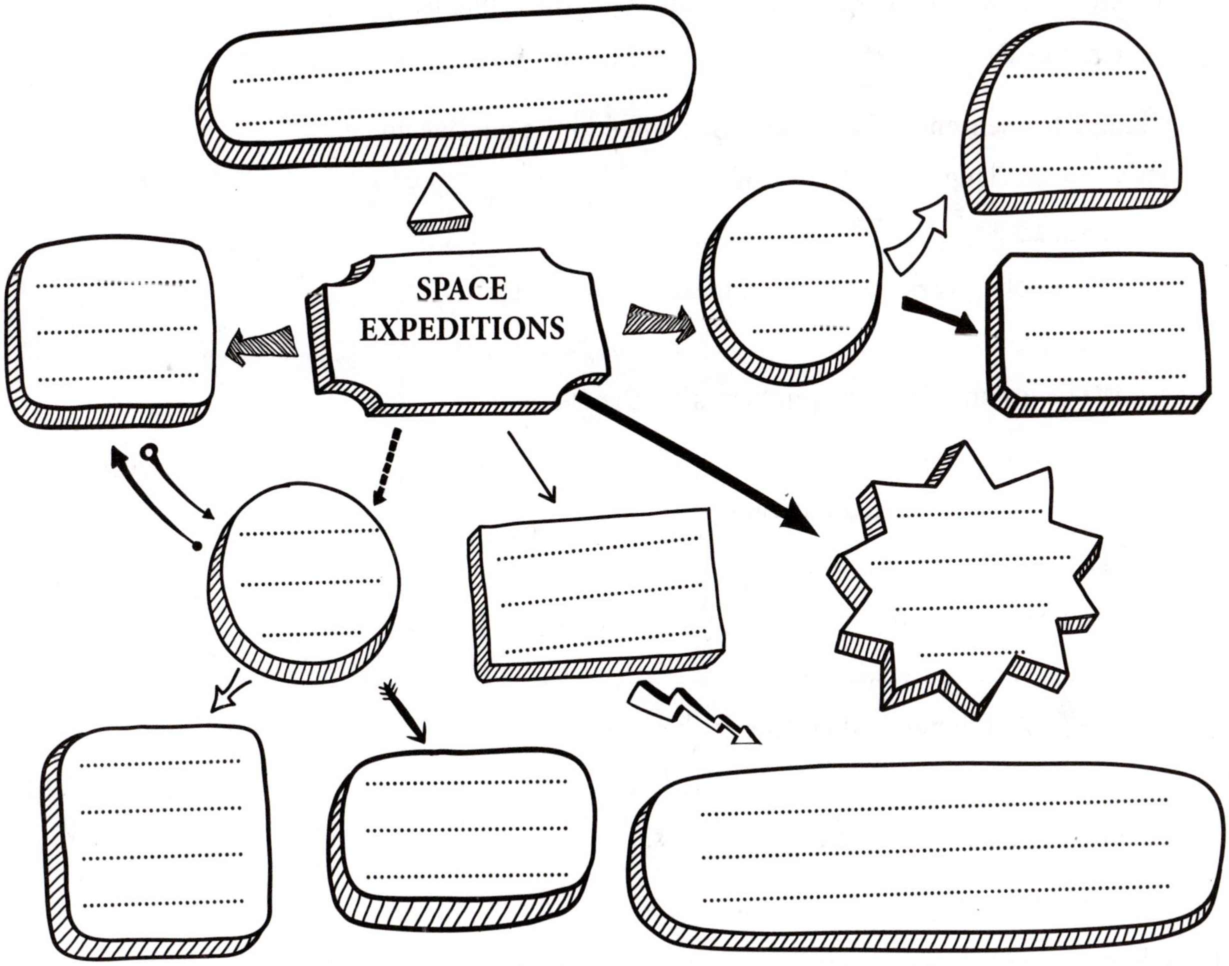


# GRAMMAR

## Active and Passive Voice

- When the doer of the action is the subject, the sentence is in the **active voice.**
- When the recipient of the action of the verb is the subject, the sentence is in the **passive voice.** For example:

    *Jerry teased Tom. (active)*
    *Tom was teased by Jerry. (passive)*
    *Children love the cartoon channel. (active)*
    *The cartoon channel is loved by children. (passive)*

**A. Underline the verbs and state whether they are in the active (A) or passive (P) voice.**

1. He had not taken the lift to his apartment. ☐
2. The choir is singing a song in the talent show. ☐
3. A game of chess can be won with proper strategy. ☐
4. The pug marks of a tiger had been seen by the hunters. ☐
5. The tourists call Kodaikanal a walker's paradise. ☐
6. Gulliver was being regarded as a small pet by the giants. ☐
7. Charles Dickens wrote the novel *David Copperfield*. ☐

**B. Change the sentences from the active voice to the passive voice.**

1. Everyone laughed at the clown's funny tricks.

 ..................................................................................................

2. The acrobat was performing trapeze acts in the circus.

 ..................................................................................................

3. We have completed our purchases for the trek.

 ..................................................................................................

4. You must have missed the train.

 ..................................................................................................

5. The teacher would have discussed these topics in the class.

 ..................................................................................................

6. The forgetful man had lost his car keys.

 ..................................................................................................

7. Old people usually avoid noisy places.

 ..................................................................................................

**C. Change the sentences from the passive voice to the active voice.**

1. Stories were being narrated by Rohan's grandmother to the children.

 ..................................................................................................

2. Heavy bags are carried by children to school.

 ..................................................................................................

3. I was scared by a squeaky sound last night.

 ..................................................................................................

4. Income tax would have been paid by the people within March.

 ..................................................................................................

5. Several new books have been bought by me.

........................................................................................................................

6. Computers must be used by people for flawless work.

........................................................................................................................

7. Seeds of different plants had been sown by the gardener.

........................................................................................................................

## *If* Conditionals

- The sentences beginning with *if* express a condition based on which the rest of the action in the sentence follows. Such sentences are described as **conditionals** or **conditional sentences**.
- In **first conditional sentences**, the possibility of the condition being fulfilled is very high. First conditionals have the structure: *if + simple present (condition), will + verb (result)*

  For example: *If we reach on time, we will get tickets to the movie.*
- In **second conditional sentences**, it is possible to fulfil the condition, but it is unlikely to happen. Second conditionals have the structure: *if + simple past (condition), would + verb (result)*

  For example: *If I knew where the sewing kit was, I would mend this hole in my sock.*
- In **third conditional sentences**, there is no possibility of the condition being fulfilled as it refers to the past. Third conditionals have the structure: *if + past perfect (condition), would have + past participle (result)*

  For example: *If you had not had the ice cream, you would not have sore throat now.*

**D. Complete the sentences with appropriate *if* conditionals.**

1. If there is a holiday today, ........................................................................................
2. If I were rich, I ........................................................................................
3. If I were a cloud, I ........................................................................................
4. If I can collect enough money, ........................................................................................
5. If I score good grades, my mother ........................................................................................
6. If the rivers swell up due to excessive rain, ........................................................................................

## *If only* and *I wish*

- *I wish* and *if only* are used to express dissatisfaction or regret because of a present or past condition that cannot be changed.
- They are also used to express hope that the condition would change in the present situation.
- The verb *be* always takes the *were* form in this type of sentences. For example:

  *If only I were there to help him.*
  *I wish I were there to help him.*

**E. Read the situations and make sentences with *I wish* or *if only*.**

1. You have forgotten to take the key to the main door of your house and now, find it shut, and you are unable to get in.

   .......................................................................................................

   .......................................................................................................

2. You have missed your school bus and are waiting for public transport.

   .......................................................................................................

   .......................................................................................................

3. You made a silly mistake in your mathematics exam, because of which you missed scoring the highest marks in the class test.

   .......................................................................................................

   .......................................................................................................

4. You have not been successful in the audition of the play to be performed in your school.

   .......................................................................................................

   .......................................................................................................

5. You have fallen sick and cannot attend your best friend's birthday party.

   .......................................................................................................

   .......................................................................................................

## Conditional sentences without *if*

- It is possible to write conditional sentences without *if* too.
- We use words like *had, provided, in case* and *unless* instead of *if*. For example:

  *If I had understood the importance of swimming, I would have started learning it from my childhood.*
  *Had I understood the importance of swimming, I would have started learning it from my childhood.*

  *If we do not take care of stray animals, they will keep suffering.*
  *Unless we take care of stray animals, they will keep suffering.*

**F. Rewrite these conditional sentences without using *if*.**

1. If you meet Purvi, please give her this book.

   .......................................................................................................

2. I could buy a new sports kit if I had more pocket money.

   .......................................................................................................

3. If the puppy does not belong to anyone else, you may keep it as a pet.

   .......................................................................................................

4. If you knew how untrustworthy he was, you would not have lent him the money.

..........................................................................................................................

5. If you do not leave now, you will get drenched in the rain.

..........................................................................................................................

6. If Komal does not practise singing regularly, she will not be able to participate in the state-level competition.

..........................................................................................................................

# LISTENING AND SPEAKING

## Speaking

### Narrating an Incident

When we narrate an incident which took place in the past, we use these tenses:

- Simple past: *We went to see a horror movie last Saturday.*
- Past continuous: *The monster was howling eerily.*
- Past perfect: *We had left home after sundown.*
- Past perfect continuous: *We had been waiting in the queue for tickets, when we heard a commotion nearby.*

**Use appropriate narrative tenses to talk about any one of these incidents.**

- A visit to an old age home
- A funny incident that happened on a trip to the museum
- One dark, stormy night, when you were home alone

# WRITING

### Diary Entry

- A **diary entry** is a first-person record of events, thoughts and feelings which the writer experiences throughout any particular day.
- For making a diary entry, keep these points in mind.
  - It is written in a conversational style and includes brief, vivid descriptions.
  - It is most often written in the simple past, present perfect, or simple future tense.
  - The date of the entry is always mentioned on the top left of the page.

**Imagine you are Neil Armstrong, and you have just returned to Earth after the first moon landing. Write a diary entry, expressing your feelings and experiences after stepping on the moon for the very first time.**

Dear Diary,

# 15 Star Trek - The Voyage Home

## VOCABULARY

### Oxymoron

- An **oxymoron** is a figure of speech in which two words, often opposite in meaning, are placed side by side, to add emphasis to the person or thing being described.
- They are commonly used to lend depth and impart a dramatic effect. For example:

  *partially empty* *audible silence* *white darkness*
  *big baby* *quiet noise*

**A. Fill in the blanks with the correct options.**

*abnormally normal* *alone together* *audible silence* *carefully casual*
*honest liar* *only option* *pretty ugly* *same difference*

1. The model set her hair in a .................................................. style.
2. Though he cheats people, he is an .................................................. .
3. She was aware of an .................................................. in the lonely house.
4. The two persons were .................................................. in the woods.
5. Though she was disturbed by the incident, she acted .................................................. .
6. The twins showed the .................................................. in their work, as in their personalities.
7. Leaving the town to start a new life was his .................................................. .
8. The witch, with her green hair and moles, appeared to be .................................................. .

B. **Match the words in Column A with those in Column B to make suitable oxymorons.**

| Column A | Column B | Oxymoron |
|---|---|---|
| 1. expressive | a. darkness | .................................. |
| 2. fully | b. death | .................................. |
| 3. living | c. empty | .................................. |
| 4. open | d. irregular | .................................. |
| 5. quiet | e. noise | .................................. |
| 6. regularly | f. secret | .................................. |
| 7. visible | g. silence | .................................. |

# LISTENING AND SPEAKING

## Speaking

### Dialogue

- A **dialogue** is a conversation between two people on any general or specific topic.
- It can be both formal or informal in tone.
- You can develop a dialogue by asking questions like *what, where, why, when* and *how*, about the topic or event, and also by using greetings.

**Work in pairs. Imagine that you are meeting your cousin, who lives abroad, after several years. You are glad to see him/her. Enact the situation. You can use these expressions.**

- How have you been?
- It's been so long.
- What have you been doing?
- It's so good to meet you finally!
- Same here, how about you?
- Have you heard/seen...?

# TEST 6

(20 marks)

## VOCABULARY ........................................................................................(5)

**Complete the crossword with the given hints.**

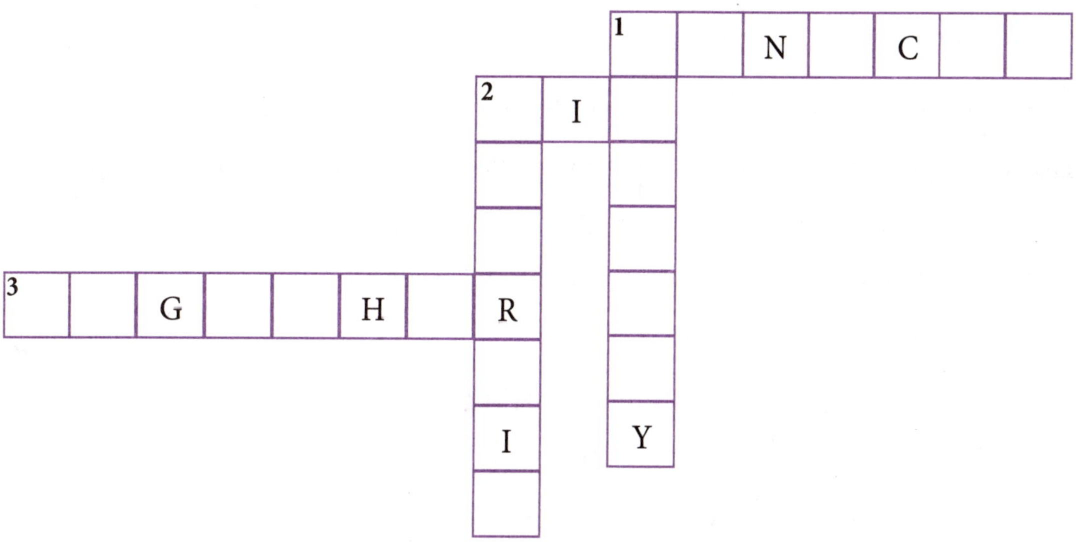


**Across**

1. remedy for all diseases
2. verb form of the word *air*
3. an oxymoron formed with the word *alone*

**Down**

1. adverb formed by adding suffix to the word *private*
2. a robot that looks like a human

## GRAMMAR ........................................................................................(10)

**A. Match the clauses to make sentences and state whether they are Main or Subordinate Clause.** **(3)**

1. To admit one's fault ..............................
2. Tea and coffee are favourite drinks ..............................
3. If the train is on time ..............................

a. which are drunk by people all over the world.

..............................................................................................

b. I will be there at the station to receive you.

..............................................................................................

c. is not easy

..............................................................................................

**B. Rewrite the sentences changing their voice. Write in the brackets whether the sentences you have made are in Active or Passive Voice.** **(3)**

1. The trapeze acts have always been considered very thrilling and dangerous by the spectators.

   ........................................................................................ (.............................................)

2. Teenagers should be paid pocket money by their parents.

   ........................................................................................ (.............................................)

3. The children are enjoying a swim in the heat.

   ........................................................................................ (.............................................)

**C. Identify the part of speech of the words in italics in the sentences below.** **(2)**

1. Do not *pepper* the chicken preparation as *pepper* will not agree with the recipe.

   ......................... .........................

2. With a *grave* and tearful face, she lay flowers on the *grave*.

   ......................... .........................

**D. Make sentences with *If* conditionals on the ideas given below.** **(2)**

1. not wake up immediately; cat; lap up the milk

   ..................................................................................................................................................

2. deep desire to have ice-cream; have no money; expressing regret

   ..................................................................................................................................................

## WRITING..........................................................................................................(5)

**A. Your school has made arrangements to present gifts to the children in an orphanage. You are a part of the group that has visited the orphanage. Write a report on this visit for your school magazine.** **(2)**

**B. You had your first public solo musical performance at the annual talent show hosted in your neighbourhood. Write a diary entry, talking about how you felt going up on the stage; which song you chose to sing; the audience's reaction to your singing; and what you are looking forward to.** **(3)**